THE

RE-START

PRINCIPLE

By
Lou Ellen Hoffman

THE RE-START PRINCIPLE

by Lou Ellen Hoffman

Copyright © 2018 by Lou Ellen Hoffman

ISBN: 978-0-9835857-7-0

Published by Spring Mill Publishing

Sharpsburg, Maryland 21782 USA

Editing by Jim Bryson (JamesLBryson@gmail.com)

Graphics by Amani Hanson (AmaniHanson.com)

Layout by Jacqueline Bryson (JacBryson@yahoo.com)

i

Endorsements

Just wanted to share briefly how your book, *The Re-Start Principle,* has helped me. About a week ago, I was in deep discouragement. I had several experiences that made me question how much faith I really had in God. I felt like my joy had been stolen. I had a lot of self-condemnation. I just couldn't get back in touch with the Holy Spirit that I felt so strongly just days before. I had no idea what was going on.

One evening, I felt the Spirit leading me to pick up your book. Re-reading the principle of aligning our soul and body with our spirit, I felt as though a life ring had been thrown to me as I was drowning in a stormy sea. Today, I am learning to be more sensitive to the Holy Spirit and to push into God.

I know your book will be a blessing to many people who know God but feel so lost and discouraged. It will be the hand they need to pull them out of their troubles.

Lauren Winters, BA, RN, RCES
Registered Nurse, Registered Cardiovascular
Electrophysiology Specialist

*****

Lou Ellen Hoffman hits the nail on the head with *The Re-Start Principle.* The revelation she brings forth is priceless to the Church in this hour. In this new millennium we the church need to Re-Start so that we can get back to our first love.

Thank you, Pastor Lou Ellen, for you your gift to the Body of Christ.

Jimmy Kellett
Prophet, Christian International Ministries Network

*****

The Re-Start Principle speaks of the love and compassion that Lou Hoffman carries for the body of Christ to come to the knowledge of the truth of Christ and what He did for us at salvation, water baptism, and baptism of the Holy Spirit.

It speaks to the church, the body of believers, why prayers are not being answered, why we don't hear God, and why we are not walking in the power of the Holy Spirit.

I highly encourage you to open your heart and understanding to the wisdom of this book. My own spiritual growth has been greatly enhanced by Pastor Lou's leadership and by this book.

Cynthia Thompson, BS
Behavioral Studies, Social Worker to the Elderly

*****

Having known Pastor Lou Ellen Hoffman for more than 30 plus years, I can tell you she hears from the Lord. That is why it is with great honor that I highly recommend her new book, *The Re-Start Principle*. I believe it has the potential to become your personal road map to living a life that is victorious. If you're fed up with being a "Yo-yo Christian," then please dive into this book and allow the revelatory truths of God's word transform your life and bring stability.

Rich Denham
Elder, Living Word Kingdom Ministries
Electric Serviceman, Mississippi Power Company

DEDICATION

To Father God, who is always speaking and showering His love on us!

To my husband, Bill who has faithfully supported me as a woman pastor, even when it wasn't popular!

To my precious children, Jason, Tammy, & Bill, Jr., who have given me love and encouragement in every phase of life.

To my parents, who loved Christ Jesus with all of their hearts, and taught Gay, Diane, Martha, Don, Lois, and me how to live and walk out our salvation in Christ, and how to love everyone, regardless of gender, race, rich or poor.

ACKNOWLEDGMENTS

To that band of faithful warriors who backed me and submitted themselves to the instruction of "practical training and activations" in following the Spirit.

Your loyalty, commitment, and dedication to the Lord and to me still move me deeply now and forever. You are so loved!

Your mandate and mission are to carry the vision the Lord has placed in all of our hearts—to train and equip the body of believers in the earth so that Kingdom advancement in the earth will be established for the return of our Lord and Savior, Christ Jesus!

CONTENTS

FOREWORD

Vince Lombardi, the winningest coach in the history of football, was known for training his teams starting at the fundamental level. When his team, the Green Bay Packers, lost the Championship the year before, he began the next season's training at the most basic level possible. Holding out a pigskin before his team of seasoned veterans, many who had played the game for years, he famously said:

"Gentlemen, this is a football."

In like manner, Lou Hoffman takes Christians back to a needed reexamination of the fundamentals of their beliefs regarding salvation, baptism, and Holy Spirit.

It doesn't get any simpler than that.

Of course, Lou has her reasons for doing this. As a pastor for over 20 years, she has seen the best and worst that the Body of Christ can experience—the highs and lows, the successes of one week followed by the tragic failures the next week. As one who gives her life for her flock—Lou has been a female pastor long before it was accepted or popular—she bleeds when the sheep bleed. Their breath is her breath. Their lives are her life. Her passion is to see the Church established in power and direction, a potent force both within as a living organism that thrives on the Word of God, and a force outward, bringing life and hope to an un-regenerated civilization that regards Christianity as weakness at best, a collection of fairytales at worst, or a mild distraction from "reality."

Lou's deepest concerns, however, are for those who say they are Christians—perhaps even meaning to be Christians— but whose lives fall far short of displaying the image of Christ in the name of the Father. It is these who apparently want more of God, who want consistency, stability, and spiritual prosperity, but fail time and time again. In the end, they can only ask, "Why? Why can't we walk with God the way we know we should? What is missing?"

What is missing is a fundamental understanding of who we are as believers, as humans, as Christians—as those who have bowed their knee at the cross of Christ and embraced the gospel message. In their headlong race toward images of glory, they've missed a thing or two along the way. Lou's book, *The Re-Start Principle*, is the launch of that much-needed turnaround, starting at the beginning—re-starting at the beginning.

Whether you are a seasoned Christian with your spiritual cruise control on "Drive," a fledgling Christian finding your way amidst the morass of contradictory messages, aims and appeals, or a mid-life Christian once strong but now weak and doubting, *The Restart Principle* has something for you. Consider it a manual of Christian mechanics, the nuts and bolts of spiritual living starting with the basics.

And yet, this work is more than a discussion. Much more. The activation exercises contained herein actually take you through the process of realigning your life with the life of God. It is the process God intended when He promised to remake you as you turned your heart to His at salvation.

There is an end to your striving, to your past mistakes and failings, to your best-laid plans coming apart at the worst possible moments. There is a solution to your struggle, water for your thirst, sustenance for your hunger, and rest for your weary soul.

It starts here.

"Ladies and Gentlemen, this is the Word of God."

INTRODUCTION

Do not call to mind the former things, or ponder things of the past. [19]Behold, I will do something new, now it will spring forth; will you not be aware of it? I will even make a roadway in the wilderness, rivers in the desert.

Isaiah 43:18-19 (NASB)

(Read this chapter all the way to the end so you won't miss the main point. This is not just another story about someone's personal life.)

It seems as if I have been in *church* all my life. My platform ministry began at the age of thirteen years old. That summer I taught myself how to play the organ. You see, our small church had no musicians. It felt right! It felt as if I was at home. I never left the platform until many, many, years later after God called me to preach.

As a young girl, my parents had begun attending a small work in Pascagoula, Mississippi. Dad helped build churches from small congregations to larger congregations. No, he didn't have a title! He wasn't a pastor, elder, or deacon. He led the singing and just loved God and people. In religious language, he would have held the title of a *layperson*. Sounds horrible now even as it is being read. Exactly what is a layperson? There is no such person described as this according to the scriptures. (The term popped up around the 15th century[1])

Dad was amazing! Many times, he would stand up in a service and give a word from the Lord. Visions were a common occurrence for him. As a girl growing up in a family of six kids,

---

[1] *The Making of a Leader, c1988 by Frank Damazio, Published by Bible Temple Publishing, p 12, "Laity & Ministry"*

we would sit around him on the bed before going to our own beds, and we would listen to him as he described what he had seen or was seeing in the spiritual realm. (Hebrews 11:3; Amos 3:7; Ephesians 6:12) He saw angels! He saw demons! He saw Jesus! My point is he *saw* into the invisible world.

So can you.

A hunger for the things of the Spirit began in my heart as that young girl growing into adulthood. Jesus became for me: *"a friend that sticks closer than a brother."* (Proverbs. 18:24) Questions began to appear in my thoughts. "How did Dad and Mom get to this place in the Spirit that allowed the supernatural to be a consistent happening in their life? What were they doing, or practicing, that caused them to be able to turn the other cheek, to have this joy, to see angels, etc., and possess this incredible love that was given to *all* people?"

My brother, Don, gave me some insight into these questions. "Lou Ellen, spiritual growth is not automatic! It takes time. It is a process. There is a difference in physical growth of the human body and spiritual growth."

The physical human body doesn't have to do anything to grow. (Other than feed it with food, water, and exercise, of course.) The body is designed to grow each year until fully developed.

Spiritual growth, on the other hand, needs to be developed! Every believer should become an initiator! Believers need to engage in spiritual activities and training or spiritual growth doesn't happen. You can't just read a book and grow! It takes training—actively engaging in spiritual exercises.

My parents taught me how to love people. Let me just say that if you don't love people then the love of Jesus is not in you. *"God is love"*! (1 John. 4:8) Jesus loved people more than anything, except of course His Father Yahweh. If you want to impact people in life, then love! *To the degree that you love, is the degree that you advance in the levels of the Kingdom of God!*

> *You can tell people anything as long as they know you love them.*

Let me say this: *ministry is all about people!* If you do not develop relationships with people and care about them genuinely, you will never progress in the Kingdom of God. Here is what I learned from my parents as they taught me by their Love for ministry and people. My motto for life is "You can tell people anything—share, instruct, correct—as long as they know you love them."

Love was manifested through my parents by their smiles and hugs for everyone, and their service in what we know as the church. This was viewed as "being a servant" for the Lord. There was no task beneath them. If the church needed cleaning, it got done. Whatever they were called on to do, it was done with joy and love. They were true ministers of the gospel. This sounds like a place we would all love to return to, doesn't it?

Mom cooked, and boy was she a good cook. She was known for her famous seafood gumbo. She never wanted to see anyone go hungry. Every preacher who came through the church came to our house to eat. Mom fed the homeless and reached out to others in need.

Dad worked at the shipyard, and his testimony was shared with those people that the Holy Spirit put in his path. He was extremely sensitive to the voice of God, and he listened closely to the directions given by the Holy Spirit. (More on this later.) Many times, people would come and tell Dad that after he prayed for them, they had become well, the pain left their bodies, or their circumstances changed.

One time, he told us the story of a co-worker who had a large growth right in the middle of his forehead. One day dad asked the man if he wanted to see that growth gone. He said, "Yes!" My dad put his finger on the growth and commanded it to dry up from the root and fall off. A few days later, the man came back very excited, saying, "Look Mr. Dees! It fell off just like you told it to do." They rejoiced together at the great thing God had done for him. Of course, being the kind of man Dad was, all the glory went to Christ! The life of my dad imitated the life of Christ! This was just one of the many, many healings that were produced through the life of my dad.

My mother also had a prophetic voice. She heard from the Lord for people and the corporate body (church) on a regular basis. She gave insight, instruction, and direction to people.

The Dees family was at church every time the door opened, which was a lot more frequent than today. In those days, people did the following:

- Worked together toward a common goal with the other Christian brothers and sisters.
- Visited the sick, shut in's, hospitals, and the prison.
- Knocked on doors and met people and prayed with them for salvation. (a thing of the past in this generation)
- Met regularly with the brothers and the sisters and fellowshipped, prayed together, and watched heaven come down.
- Shared their testimony everywhere they went.

Mom and Dad were passionate, vibrant, loving, servants of the Most High God until they went to be with Jesus. I said *until*. Do you get the point? They lived the gospel out in their daily lives until...they left this earth for a better place called heaven. They knew who they were in Christ! Hearing the voice of God was no problem for them! Knowing their redemptive[2] and spiritual gifts[3] and the gifts flowing in and through them was not an issue! They walked in victory with the joy and peace of God on their lives.

What Am I Describing?

I know you want that in your life today—sharing, teaching, prophesying, healing the sick, serving people, being a leader, giving a word of encouragement to someone, showing mercy, being a giver, yes even casting out demons and having visions and dreams of the invisible world.

The *real deal*! Yes! I am describing something that sounds so unlike what we are seeing in today's church. There was a deep, deep hunger in me for something more than just going to church. I wanted to *be* the church in the way the church is presented in the Bible.

My heart began to question:

- Why would Jesus allow the Holy Scriptures to describe living victoriously instead of defeated?
- How did the disciples endure persecution and evidential death, yet remain filled with joy and peace?
- Did God mean what He said to us in scriptures or not? Can we actually imitate Him?[4]

Then I realized that He intends for us to live a victorious life through *all* hardships, *all* obstacles, and *all* pain and suffering. The Bible is the inspired, infallible[5], (not capable of being wrong

---

[2] *Romans 12:6-8, 1 Peter 4:10*
[3] *1 Corinthians 12:4, 5, 8-10*
[4] *Ephesians 5:1 (NASB) "Therefore be imitators of God, as beloved children;"*
[5] *www.merriam-webster.com/dictionary/infallible*

or making mistakes) Word of God[6].

My parents modeled a lifestyle of living the Gospel daily through our Lord Jesus Christ, living lives full of love but also full of signs and wonders, and yes, even miracles. They experienced the trials of life in *peace* and *joy*! Yes, there were hardships, but they sailed through them by knowing and living Christ!

Over twenty years of being a pastor at one church has shown me many things. There have been many up and down growth spurts. In one week, we might have an increase of people who joined our fellowship, and the next week, the same number leave! There is nothing we haven't attempted in fellowships, events, activities for kids, adults, community outreaches, revivals, or training. You name it! We offered it! Still, the Kingdom of God was not expanded according to Genesis 1:27-28.

Many hours of prayer and years later, the Lord began to open my spirit to the answer. This book is the product of what Father God, through our precious Holy Spirit, began to speak to me.

This book is not an attempt to rewrite what many others have written about so wonderfully concerning the church, the present-day movement of the apostolic, and the re-aligning of the government of God with the fivefold ministry. Rather, it is an attempt to open people's eyes to truth that is being presented in this age in which we are living. I recommend catching up if you are behind in what God is doing now!

The mind is a strange animal. It has so many thoughts, desires, and attempts to figure life out by reasoning and deductions. Unfortunately, the gospel of Jesus Christ doesn't

---

[6] *New Life Version (NLV) Copyright © 1969 by Christian Literature International*

work very well in this manner. The things of God are not understood by the natural mind.

> *But a natural man does not accept the things of*
> *the Spirit of God, for they are foolishness to him;*
> *and he cannot understand them, because they*
> *are spiritually appraised.*

1 Corinthians 2:14 (NASB)

I am asking you to open your eyes and heart to see and hear what the Spirit has to say to us in the here and now.

Keep reading and let the Holy Spirit—our Comforter, Teacher, and Guide[7]—speak to you. Then activate yourself in what you have read by *doing*!

Are you ready to move beyond your present place in the Kingdom?

Then let's get *started*!

---

[7] *KJV, (King James Version) Holy Bible John 14:26*

1

WHAT IS THE SALVATION RE-START PRINCIPLE?

For God so loved the world, that He gave His only begotten Son, that whoever believes in Him shall not perish, but have eternal life.

John 3:16 (NASB)

"Re-Start"[8] is defined as the following:

- To start anew.
- To resume something, such as an activity) after interruption.
- To resume operation.

"Principle"[9] is defined as the following:

- A moral rule or belief that helps you know what is right and wrong and that influences your actions.
- A rule or code of conduct.
- A law or fact of nature that explains how something works or why something happens.

All of these definitions can speak to us in our Christian walk of life. Think and meditate on the definitions above! You decide if there are things in your Christian life that are no longer working or maybe you don't have the knowledge or understanding about them. Is your present Christian walk as a

---

[8] *https://www.merriam-webster.com/dictionary/restart*
[9] *https://www.merriam-webster.com/dictionary/principle*

believer of Yeshua, Jesus, enough?

To answer that question, ask yourself:

- Do I hear the voice of God on a consistent basis? Do I know His voice? Can I know when it is God's voice, satan's voice, or my own human reasoning voice?[10]
- Can I tell when it is satan's voice (he is not deserving of a capital "S" grammatically) speaking to me, God speaking, or if it is my own human voice?
- Who am I in Christ? Do I identify with Him or do I still think I am (*insert your full name*)? If my identity is in myself then there is a major problem in my Christian walk.
- Am I full to overflowing of the Holy Spirit? Does the fruit of the Spirit flow through me on a consistent everyday basis? Or am I full of discouragement, pain, sickness, and sadness? (You get my drift.)

If we admit it, all of us at times in our walk with the Lord realize that we are missing something. Some of us realize that going to church, listening to a message, or even reading our Bible isn't scratching the itch that is on the inside of us. We sense we have missed something or that there is more—something important about the kingdom because we are not manifesting the fruit of the Spirit.

> *But the fruit of the Spirit is love, joy, peace, patience, kindness, goodness, faithfulness, [23]gentleness, self-control; against such things there is no law.*
>
> Galatians 5:22-23 (NASB)

---

[10] *There are three voices that can speak to you: 1) God's voice 2) satan's voice, and 3) your own human reasoning voice*

Unfortunately, there are many believers who are struggling today with the church as they know it. Many believe that something is missing in their walk with the Lord Jesus.

What Is Missing?

Is it possible that when Jesus *Re-lifed* me in salvation, as I accepted Him as Lord of my life, that I missed something vitally important in my transition to the next step in the life of a new believer in Him?

Water baptism is the next step in our walk in Christ! Again, is it possible that there is more we need to know to progress as believers, rather than acting out what Jesus did for us through His death, burial, and resurrection? Is there more than just going through the ritual we now have in the church? Is there something important to take away from this experience?

As new believers, we might find ourselves moving toward the baptism of the Holy Spirit! We might say, "I don't believe in tongues!" Well, we may not believe in tongues but I'm sure we believe in being "full of the Holy Spirit." After all, we received Him in salvation! We might question:

- Does He just sit there inside of us doing nothing?
- Is there more to this Holy Spirit than what I know?
- Can I empty out of the Holy Spirit?
- Should I want to be full of Him, the third person of the Godhead?
- What is the purpose of Him?
- Why can't I get by without Him?

Most believers in the Kingdom of God today do not understand this principle of the Holy Spirit fullness. If we don't understand it, then how can we help enlarge the Kingdom of

3

God in the earth today? Perhaps we did not learn the truth or principle of what it means to be *full* of the Holy Spirit.

What is so important about salvation, water baptism, and Holy Spirit baptism? What are the steps and actions that we may have missed in each one of these important places in our lives?

I meet people all the time who tell me that they never hear the voice of God. Have you ever had someone tell you that they don't know what their purpose in life is and they don't know how or where they fit in the Body of Christ? There are Christians everywhere who struggle with their walk in Christ! Others say, "I've been serving the Lord for years and still live at the intersection of *Barely Getting By* street and *Discouragement* avenue!

Yet the Word of God says we are to be *"more than conquerors"* (Romans. 8:37). So why are we not conquerors?

The reason there is so much discouragement, lack of passion, and despair in the body of believers is that we have not understood the importance of the basic steps or principles of our salvation, water baptism, and Holy Spirit baptism. There are key principles that we have missed!

(Please hang in here with me! Don't stop reading now.)

The Bottom Line

Let's consider these questions:

- What truth, steps, or lessons have I missed or not learned in each phase of my salvation, water baptism and Holy Spirit baptism?
- What principles (the truth or lesson that influences our actions and behavior; a code of conduct) have I not fully and completely understood or been taught?

In my personal walk with the Lord, there were many

4

questions that were not answered until years later. Oh, how I wanted to grow, but there were no trainers!

Do you know *why* you are still feeling let down, discouraged, depressed, and going around and around the same mountain over and over again? Why are you making wrong choices and decisions? Do you want to know?

Of course, you do!

You will be surprised as we continue this journey of *The Re-Start Principle*. Let me encourage you! You are not alone in having some of the feelings above. Read along with us as we identify the lessons missed or not learned in each of these important moments in the life of every believer—new or been saved for many years.

Join us in *The Re-Start Principle* that will storm the gates of hades. (Matthew 16:18) This principle will totally transform who you are and accelerate you into the deeper levels of walking in victory.

2

<u>THE WAY IT IS</u>
<u>SUPPOSED TO WORK</u>!

Now these are the {people} <u>gifts</u> Christ <u>gave</u> to the <u>church</u>: {an assembly, congregation; Body of Christ} the <u>apostles</u>, the <u>prophets</u>, the <u>evangelists</u>, and the <u>pastor</u> {used only 1x in the NT; should be Shepherd} and <u>teachers</u>. [12]Their responsibility is to equip God's people to do his work and build up the church, the body of Christ. [13]This will continue until we all come to such unity in our faith and knowledge of God's Son that we will be mature in the Lord, measuring up to the full and complete standard of Christ. (Emphasis added)

Ephesians 4:11-13 (NLT)

Please make sure you have read the scripture above and understand what it is saying.

Now, let's look at what it is not saying. It is not saying that once you receive Christ, that you are on your own, trying to learn how to walk with Christ! It does not say that you will struggle, and struggle for years trying to figure it all out without help!

What it does say is that God has given assignments in the Body of Christ to specific members of that body to be the trainers (leaders) to the many members of the Body of Christ. (1 Corinthians 12:12-27)

They are called apostle, prophet, evangelist, pastor (shepherd) and teacher. (Ephesians 4:11-13) These gifts are given to individual people, called by God, for the specific purpose of *trainers* to prepare all believers, young and old, for works of service, and to mature and grow them up in Christ. We will refer to these trainers as *gift leaders.*

> *Most of us have only been exposed to the pastoral ministry!*

Most of us have only been exposed to one of these gift leaders in our church life. That is the role of the pastor (or shepherd). (see *The Apostolic Church Arising*[11] for present-day truth on this subject)

Each one of these gift leaders has a specific role and assignment of training for the Body of Christ. We all pretty much know what a few of these do. The pastor takes care of the people by meeting their needs of care, comfort, and protection. The teacher gives instruction and training which helps people grow up in the kingdom. The evangelist gets people saved. The apostles set the church in order and establish new works.

The issue is that we have set each one of these gift leaders as a separate part of the local body. There are many churches who do not even recognize these gifts to the Body of Christ in this present age, even though Ephesians 4:13 states: "*until we all come to the unity of the faith and of the knowledge of the Son of God, to a perfect man, to the measure of the stature of the fullness of Christ.*" (Emphasis added)

Each role and purpose of each of these gift leaders is different, as we can readily agree upon, but each of these gift leaders is given the mandate to *train and equip the body until*

---

[11] *"The Apostolic Church Arising"* by Chuck Pierce & Robert Heidler, Chapter 6, The Pastoral Model, pp. 58-62.

they are mature. They are called the governmental members of the body.

A pastor (shepherd) should be teaching and training someone else to meet the needs of people! An apostle should be teaching and training someone in the body how to become an apostle, how to start new churches, etc. An evangelist should have on-the-job training in how to preach messages along with activating the miracles, signs, and wonders that win the lost. The teacher should be instructing someone how to pull together a training session, how to organize it, etc. A prophet should be giving activations and instructions on how to prophesy. Not only do the trainers train, but they should also be actively engaged in their roles in ministry.

For further study, there are great books already defining this in great detail.

God's Plan for His Church

How can we be properly trained in our church experience if we only sit under a pastor/shepherd's or teacher's care? Pastors love to care for the sheep. But we will not grow up if someone is constantly petting us and meeting our needs. We will not progress in the Kingdom of God in this manner. The analogy of a child can be used to figure this one out for ourselves. The Word of God clearly states this:

> *Does everyone have a pastor ministry of care, and giving? Are all apostles?... Do all have gifts of healing?... but earnestly desire the most helpful gift.* (Emphasis added)

> 1 Corinthians 12:29-31

The answer is *absolutely not!*

If we have received training from only *one* of the gift people God has established in the church, such as the pastor or teacher, then it only makes sense that we might have missed some important training in our experience of salvation, water baptism, and the Holy Spirit! Father God has principles in each area of these three places in our walk that many have not known about or did not spend the necessary time in training. (We will reveal in later chapters those principles missed or not activated in our lives.)

> *Lack of training produces weak Christians!*

This lack of training is exactly what has happened for years when we assemble as the Church. It could be a symptom of Christian believers who are stunted in their growth and are just trying to hang in there hoping things will change. Lack of training produces weak Christians!

Many believers have quit attending church, and those who attend may do it out of a sense of obligation because that is what they've been taught to do. (My momma went to church, my granddad went....)

It is time to wake up as believers and align ourselves with the *government of God's order*! Every individual believer has received the same commission from Jesus as He prepared to go to heaven. We are *all* called to minister!

> *Go therefore and make disciples of all the nations, baptizing them in the name of the Father and of the Son and of the Holy Spirit, [20] teaching them to observe all things that I have commanded you; and lo, I am with you always, even to the end of the age." Amen.*
>
> Matthew 28:19-20 (NKJV)

Every believer has been called to be a minister! (Matthew 18:23; 25:19, 29; Romans 14:12) Every one of us received the same package of the Godhead—Father, Son, and Holy Spirit—into our inner man! We have everything we need to be victorious in this life we are now living.

Yet your mind is saying "But I am not a pastor! I am not a teacher! I am not …." Stop that thinking right now! You may not be a gifted leader, whose function is to train others, but each one of us has a place of ministry in the Body of Christ. (1 Corinthians 12)

Each one of us has a story to tell that will affect others. Each one of us can pray with someone or for someone's needs. A minister is not just someone who is in charge of a church. Remember we have gift leaders who have been given to the Body of Christ to train, equip, and grow up the individual members to *"do the work of the ministry."*(Ephesians 4:12) This does not mean that we should not be growing and learning how to *"sit with Him in heavenly places,"* (Ephesians 2:6), learning how to walk and stand in Christ.

3

FIRST THINGS FIRST

Nor is there salvation in any other, for there is no other name under heaven given among men by which we must be saved.

Acts 4:12 (NKJV)

Your life begins at the cross of Jesus Christ! (Acts 4:12; 1 John. 4:7-8; John 3:16) You must repent, confess, and believe in the work of Jesus Christ on the cross to enter into the Kingdom of God. Your life in the Kingdom of God begins at this point.

Some people think that salvation is only a ticket to heaven! Growing up in the church, this was the main thing I heard. "If you don't get saved and come to Jesus, then you are going to hell. You won't get to go to heaven." This was the main message taught about salvation. Some answered the call out of fear of not wanting to go to hell! Others received the call out of true godly conviction and received Christ as their Savior. Many believed that this secured a ticket to heaven and that was all that was needed.

In times past, fear was a strategy that many used to chalk up numbers on their climb to ministry success. A host of *Do Not's* was the other messages that many heard about heaven and Jesus. (I just want to fall down on my knees right now and praise the Father, Son, and Holy Spirit for the wisdom, insight and the revelation that is being given in this day and age in which we are living.)

> *Is salvation more than just a ticket to heaven?*

Salvation is more than just a ticket to heaven. (Thank you, Jesus, for that ticket to heaven, but thank you, Jesus, because there is so much more.)

Salvation gives me eternal life. When my physical body dies, my spirit lives forever in that invisible, unseen dimension or world. (John 3:16; Colossians 1:16-17; Hebrews 11:13)

Realizing there is more than just a ticket to heaven opens up an entirely new line of thought processes. If there is more to salvation than just getting my ticket to heaven in the sweet bye-and-bye, then what more did I received? (I'll address this in a later chapter.)

The Point

We need to re-define and *Re-Start* ourselves from the point of salvation and discover what principles are missing that have prevented us from becoming all that the Bible promises.

As Jesus comes in and *Re-life's* us on the inside, our desires will change for the better and our very nature will transform. This act of bringing back to life our dead spirits is a *Re-Start* process. The process of salvation and deliverance from sin and its consequences causes our old nature (ugly attitudes, actions, and behaviors) to begin to conform to the image of Christ. We begin to look more like Jesus. (Romans 12:2; Colossians 1:16; 1 Corinthians 11:1)

A change in a person's nature, character, etc., is a great way to know that a person has had this experience of salvation. (It's not the only way to tell, but it's a pretty good indicator.) If the person was full of anger, you will see a change to calmness and peace. Things won't upset them like they use to do. If the person

14

was hateful and ugly, then you will see a change in their nature to one of love and kindness. Remember, change from the old nature may take time, but for the most part, you will see a significant change immediately.

The decision to choose Christ is the most important decision of anyone's life. Yet, I've seen people who were saved one day and lost the next day. The Bible says, *"A double minded man is unstable in all his ways."* (James 1:8 KJV)

Double-minded is defined as:

1) wavering in mind: undecided, vacillating
2) marked by hypocrisy: insecure.

(Merriam-Webster online dictionary)

Truth #1

You must have your foot on the rock and your mind made up! No turning back!

Choosing Christ is a forever decision! Not *on* one day and *off* the next. It is a forever decision! Do not take it lightly! Make up your mind right now to choose Christ for life. Believe me, you will experience life to its fullest.

If you are a believer who is living beneath your inheritance in Christ right now, you have an opportunity to *Re-Start* your salvation and grow in the areas mentioned later in this book. If you have never confessed Jesus as Lord of your life, then today can be the beginning of a new start in your life!

Once you are in Christ, you can begin to grow! The *Re-Start principle* works for everyone—a new believer or one who has already accepted Christ. Use the prayer called, *Activation Prayer*, below.

Say it out loud where you can hear yourself because, *"Faith* comes by hearing, and hearing by the word of God." (Romans 10:17 NKJV)

Activation Prayer

Prayer for New Believer

"Father God, I come to You right now, in the name of Jesus and I confess as sin that I chose the world and its way instead of You! My heart is stirred and I recognize that the life I am now living is not one of peace.

I believe that You gave Your only son, Jesus so that we may have everlasting life (John 3:16). I receive the life of my spirit man into eternal life.

I confess with my mouth that Jesus is my Lord and I believe in my heart that God raised Jesus from the dead. (Romans 10:9-10)

Today is a new day with Christ! I choose this day to live for You and will follow You to the best of my abilities, never looking back. You are my life. Teach me Your ways! I commit myself to actively train for the Kingdom of God in the name of Jesus. Amen!

Prayer for A Believer to Re-Start

Father God, create in me a clean heart and a right spirit. (Psalm 51:10) Help me turn from my past life of living as a son or daughter on Barely-Getting- By-Street, which has followed me into my present mode of living.

My heart is stirred to think that there is a way to live for You that is not just a religious form. It stops here and now! I choose to follow You! I commit myself to actively train for the Kingdom of God instead of only attending church and listening.

Teach me Your path, Your ways, and the principles that have been hidden in plain sight, so that I might be an effective believer in this present world. Show me the things that I have not fully learned about You and the Kingdom of God, so that I may grow up in You in love and become a mature member of the Body of Christ. (Ephesians 4:15)

Help me to move to the next level in the Kingdom of God in the here and now, only after training in the truth that I have missed. Thank You for Your forgiveness, love, and strength to move forward! In the name of Jesus, Amen!

4

THE REVELATION

And I also say to you that you are Peter, and on this rock I will build My church, and the gates of Hades shall not prevail against it.

Matthew 16:18 (NKJV)

In the last chapter, we talked about not being a double-minded person. Stability is so needed in the Body of Christ today! There is too much "on and off" in Christianity. No wonder unbelievers look upon the church and turn away!

The Holy Spirit began to deal with me about the lack of spiritual progress in Christians. The burden that I began to have for the church was weighing me down. Most of my life had been spent in the church. I could remember the days of excitement, people coming to Jesus, miracles happening, incredible joy in the midst of trouble and despair, and people who loved.

More and more, God's people began to display behaviors that were more like the Israelite children who were in bondage: griping, complaining, no peace, no victory, no joy in living, etc. Somewhere along the way things changed. No longer was it a privilege and joy to attend the house of the Lord. We already knew what we would receive. More of the same, over and over—grumblings and what we call "drama" today. So much division and a lack of love!

When I told my dad at the age of forty-five that the Lord had called me to preach His Word, he said, "Lou Ellen, whatever you do, don't bore them to death." (I laughed.)

Boredom! Lack of present-day truth!

A cry began to come from my heart: "Lord, show me what is wrong with the present-day church." Thank the Lord that as I began to shift some things around in my own life, He began to reveal the truth to me little-by-little. (Isaiah 28:10. This is the scripture that I live by!)

As my husband, Bill, and I were traveling to church in the fall of 2017 on a Sunday morning, the Holy Spirit began to give me a download which produced this book you are reading. I grabbed my pen and a blank sheet of paper and began to write out an outline. The first thing I wrote down was salvation, then water baptism, and following that was Spirit baptism. My head was saying, "Lord, is that it? What am I going to say that will be different from the many times I have preached on salvation, water baptism, and Spirit baptism?"

He spoke to me and said, "Haven't you been praying about the spiritual condition of my Church, the Body of Christ?"

I immediately responded, "Of course."

He said, "Just begin speaking about salvation and I will give you insight as you step out in faith. I will fill your mouth."

He brought to my remembrance a few scriptures to go with the outline and somehow, I just knew that this would be another God-breathed message.

As the time to minister the Word came, I stepped up and begin to tell the people what had happened on the way to church. Suddenly, a flow of revelation and insight into how we were not trained in certain areas of our Christian walk began to flow out of my mouth. For the next five weeks, God spoke through me the revelation revealed in this book, of the spiritual condition of the body, and how re-training must take place in the heart of old and new believers.

Let us begin with Salvation!

What have we missed in our salvation experience? We received Jesus into our heart but what is the ache that has not been fulfilled? We make statements like, "I read my Bible, attend church and Bible study! What is it? Something is not working! I find myself doing things that I should not be doing, and not doing things I should." (Romans 7:15-20) Sound familiar? Don't lose heart, you are not alone in this battle. The answers are getting closer.

Three Main Keys (Principles) To Re-Start

There are three main principles in our salvation experience that we must be trained in until they become a part of us. If you are a new believer then this will be a lot easier because you don't have to go back and *Re-Start*. For those who have been in church for a longer period of time, it will take some work. We can be so stuck in what we have previously known.

Training means that we must do something! We have a part to play beyond sitting in church listening to a message. We must actively engage and take the time to train, acquiring the skill and knowledge that is needed.

As an existing believer, if we don't get these three principles trained into us, then there will be some major issues in our Christian walk later in life. Believe me, I know this to be true because of my own experiences. I was blind to some issues until the Holy Spirit opened my eyes and revealed the truth to me.

In the next chapter, we will list the three principles or keys of advancement that believers need. We will also look at what we are not trained to do, but depend on other ministers, evangelists, prophets, to do for us.

21

5

<u>KEYS FOR ADVANCEMENT</u>

Now may the God of peace Himself sanctify you completely; and may your whole spirit, soul, and body be preserved blameless at the coming of our Lord Jesus Christ.

1 Thessalonians 5:23 (NKJV)

I will give you the <u>keys</u> of the kingdom of heaven, and whatever you bind on earth will be bound in heaven, and whatever you loose on earth will be loosed in heaven. (Emphasis added)

Matthew 16:19 (NKJV)

The precious Holy Spirit revealed these simple but profound truths to me after many years of living and serving the Lord. There are *keys* that we have been given once we received salvation. (Matthew 16:19) Salvation is referred to in this book as receiving your ticket to heaven, and/or being *Re-lifed* in some texts. Following the instructions written in the following pages will change our lives!

Maybe you have never been taught that there are keys which will increase your walk in Christ if you know them and practice them. Right up front, it is important for every believer to know and practice these keys or principles in their life when they become "born again of the Spirit." (John 3:5-7)

- Key #1. I am a spirit, who was created with a soul, which lives in a body which makes me a three-part being of spirit, soul, and body.

- Key #2. Go inward to His presence (Spirit).
- Key #3. Hearing and recognizing the _three voices_.

These three simple principles practiced daily will become habit-forming. Learning these lessons now and activating them through practice will escalate you into the supernatural dimension of the Kingdom of God in the earth!

Please don't skip anything! Even if you think you have heard or read this before, remember that many of us have heard, these things while sitting under preachers or training classes with no practical activations—hearing but not practiced.

Every step is essential to your understanding and growth.

This first _Re-Start Principle_ is foundational to everything else you must process in your Christian walk.

6

BACK TO THE GARDEN

B. C. (Before Christ)

*And the LORD God formed man of the dust [body]
of the ground, and breathed into his nostrils the
breath of life [spirit]; and man became a living
being [soul].* (Emphasis added)

Genesis 2:7 (NKJV)

What was the original design and intent of God when He created mankind?

In the garden, before the fall of Adam and Eve, we were created a three-part being by our creator, God. This is because we are created in His image. (Genesis 1:26-27) Here is the way the scripture above describes our three-part make up.

- Part 1 "God formed man of the dust" = Outer form, our *body.*
- Part 2 "God breathed into his [man's] nostrils the breath of Life = *spirit.*
- Part 3 "Man became a living being = *soul.*

It is believed and taught by some that as soon as God breathed the breath of life into man, the soul was produced. However, it happened, we know this: The soul and the spirit were in perfect harmony and agreement in the Garden. They became one.

The number three signifies completion, perfection, and unity. Three is the number of the Godhead, the Trinity. Is it any wonder that the soul and the spirit became one in unity?

The Three-Part Make-Up of Man

(Original Design) (See Figure 1)

1. The Spirit (God) ruled.
2. The *soul* (mind, will, emotions) are submitted to the Spirit.
3. The *soul* navigates the *body.*
4. The *body* follows the instructions from the *soul.*

In this unified state, Adam and Eve were totally oblivious to their body and its outside garment of no clothing. (Genesis 2:25; 3:11)

They were clothed in garments of light (Shekinah glory of God). They walked with their daddy God in the cool of the day (Genesis 3:8) and talked with Him daily.

Everything was beautiful!

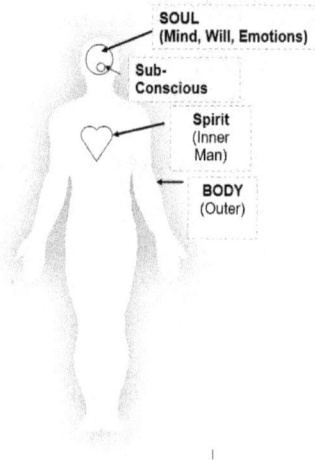

Adam was in harmony with God, which meant that his *spirit* and *soul* agreed with one another.

The *spirit* ruled and sent the instructions, (what to name the animals, etc.) to the *soul,* and the *soul* sent the signals to the *body* to carry it out. (mouth spoke)

Adam was filled with God's Word! He had knowledge of God. He walked and talked with God and fellowshipped with God.

Figure 1

God created man this way for a specific purpose! Adam and Eve knew who they were and why they were created. They knew their destiny.

Adam and Eve had the mandate to rule over, subdue, and

expand the Garden of Eden—the Kingdom of God—to the rest of the earth. (Genesis 1:28) That mandate included bringing, not just life, but abundant living and divine blessings to mankind. (John 10:10b)

That is exactly what they were doing until sin entered the picture. *Merriam-Webster Dictionary* describes sin as: "to commit an offense or fault." Others call it: "missing the mark."

Summary

First and foremost, all human beings are spirit, not just bodies. At the beginning of creation, you were created a three-part person—a spirit who possesses a soul, (mind, will, and emotions) and lives in a body. Your spirit is like God because you are created in His image. (Genesis 1:27)

What Happened A.S. (After Sin)[12]

Adam and Eve's three-part nature became out of balance after entering into agreement with the serpent in Genesis 3. When Adam sinned, he took away my choice! (Psalm 51:5) All mankind is born into sin! Adam allowed his emotions (soul) to rule on the day he and Eve ate the forbidden fruit.

Emotions will move you out of the will of God! Hear me when I say that this is the #1 enemy in the church today. Every issue of a man's life is determined by *who rules* his emotions (soul). The curse over the earth is that it is emotionally ruled.

Description of what transpired: Adam's spirit (the God part) died. A curtain dropped between the *soul* and the *spirit* (the inner man). The *spirit* (God connector) died as a result of Adam and Eve's choice.

---

[12] *A.S. (after sin) = my abbreviation*

They traded away a relationship with their Father God! No longer did they look like their daddy. Another image began to work in them. The glory and radiance of daddy God had covered them to the extent that they did not know they were naked until they agreed with the serpent!

> *Man traded Kingdom of God in the earth for the kingdom of the world.*

What did they trade? They traded the opportunity to expand this heavenly garden across the world—the Kingdom of God in the earth—for the kingdom of the world. Gloom, despair, and agony on me.

The Process

Halleluiah, Father God had a plan to buy us back from the sinful nature!

Our spirit becomes alive again or *born again* when we invite Jesus Christ to become the ruler in our lives. (John 3:16-17) The new creation in Christ spoken of in 2 Corinthians 5:17, occurs in the human spirit, not the soul or the body.

When a human being is born again, they become brand new in their *spirit*. I call it getting *Re-lifed*. Your spirit has an instant awakening and complete transformation. This means that the (God) spirit can again rule and help man live a victorious life.

Body and soul are impacted by what happens, but not completely transformed. Only your spirit is *brand new*! Remember, God rules in your spirit!

Your soul (mind, will, and emotions) and your body must now make a connection, linking up with your *Re-lifed* spirit. (See Figure 2)

The Three Parts of Man – A.S. (after Sin)

28

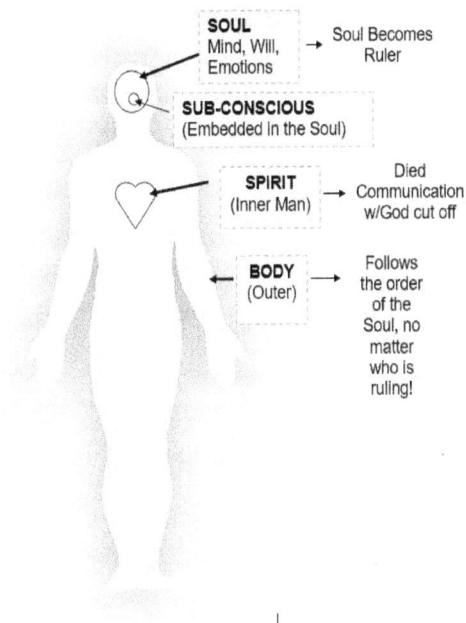

Figure 2

- The Spirit (God) dies and no longer rules.
- The *soul* (mind, will, emotions) takes *rulership.*
- The *soul* still navigates the *body.*
- The *body* follows the instructions from the *soul.*

How Does This Happen?

Transformation happens when your *soul* gets into agreement with, yields to, and surrenders to what has already transpired in your *spirit*!

Most new believers in Jesus, and many born-again believers who have served the Lord for a long time do not understand that they are a three-part human: spirit, soul, and body.

Why is this so important for every believer to know at the entry point to the Kingdom of God in salvation? Because being born again, saved, or *Re-lifed*, makes them a citizen in a Kingdom (another book for another time) and they can't advance in the

29

Kingdom unless they know how their human nature should respond to and with the God inside.

Simply stated, your spiritual growth can only take place with this *Re-Start Principle*!

Spirit is the dimension of man which operates the spiritual realm. This is the part of man that knows God. Everything that is needed to live a successful life on the earth is located here in your spirit.

This is *Re-life*, or born-again through a salvation conversion (change, transformation, metamorphosis). It is when you make Christ Lord (or ruler) of your life. This is also the part of you that longs for communion with God. You become more God-*conscious*!

Soul is the dimension of man that deals with the mental (psyche) realm. It deals with the mind, (the ability to make a decision), and emotions, (the ability for feelings).

The soul is self (flesh) conscious, self-centered, and wants to be in power all the time. Yes, even after you have submitted yourself to Christ! It is in a state of rebellion against the spirit, which is God consciousness! (Galatians 5:16-19)

Body is the outer dimension of man which functions in the physical realm. It is the house of the spirit (spiritual realm) and the soul (mental realm, your psyche), and it carries out the functions or orders from the soul (mind, will, emotions). The body has senses (sight, smell, taste, hear, and touch) and consciousness of its natural, worldly environment. It is all about what you can see, hear, touch, taste, and smell outside the body in the physical world.

It is important to read this and say it aloud!

My body is the house of the spiritual realm and the mental realm—my psyche.

As a new creation in Christ, do *not* think of yourself only as a physical being! Think of yourself as a spiritual being who can deal with the mental realm, the psyche, and that is housed in a body! That just zinged someone reading this! I felt it in my spirit! You are more than a conqueror when you yield, surrender, your soul (your flesh nature) to the spirit in your inner man.

Say this out loud!

"I am a spirit who operates a spiritual realm, who possesses, seizes, and takes control of my soul, my mind, will, reasoning, emotions, and I live in a body."

Think of yourself in this light!

For as he thinks in his heart, so is he.

Proverbs 23:7 (NKJV)

This scripture is saying that "as a man [human being] *thinks* in his heart [mind, will, emotions] so is he."

"Heart," as translated by *Strong's Concordance* H5315, is the word nephesh. Nephesh is defined as a soul, living being, life, self, person, desire, passion, appetite, or emotion.

If you think negatively of yourself, that you are only a poor human being, doing your best to get by down here on the earth, and you only have a ticket to heaven, then that is what you will become.

If you are thinking gloom, despair, and agony on me, then this type of thinking will project onto other people and it will form their opinion of you. You know this is true because you can look at a person and tell whether they are having a good day, a bad day, if they are depressed, etc.

This attitude in your soul (your mental realm) has given orders to the body to project the same attitude to the body and the body carries out the look of depression, aggravation, etc. Are you getting the picture?

A friend of mine recently taught on The Grasshopper Mentality. I believe this is an accurate scripture of how believers think at times.

> *There we saw the giants (the descendants of Anak came from the giants) and we were like grasshoppers in our own sight, and so we were in their sight.* (Emphasis added)
>
> Numbers 13:33 (NKJV)

We need to break out of the mindset that says we are poor little human beings struggling to understand our Father God, our brother, Jesus, and the precious Holy Spirit. God has created us in His image to *rule and reign* in this present life! Can I get an Amen right here?

> *Then God blessed them, and God said to them, "Be fruitful and multiply; fill the earth and subdue it; have dominion over the fish of the sea, over the birds of the air, and over every living thing that moves on the earth."* (Emphasis added)
>
> Genesis 1:28 (NKJV)

The word *dominion* is the word *rule*: "to tread down, subjugate, crumble, prevail against, reign, take."[13]

Stop for a moment and pray this prayer aloud:

"Thank you, Father God, for blessing me and giving me the ability to be fruitful and to multiply. You have given me the

---

[13] *Strong's Talking Dictionary, H7287*

mandate to fill the earth by subduing it, ruling, treading down, subjugating it, crumbling, prevailing against, reigning over, and taking back all that the enemy has stolen from me."

Can you see why it is so important to understand your three-fold nature? Spiritual growth will have been stunted and you will have wasted years of only barely getting by if you get miles down the road from your salvation to discover this *Re-start principle*! (We will practice at the end of the chapter.)

New believers—those who are just coming into the kingdom—can get this understanding of their three-part make-up right from the beginning. It is only operating *in* the kingdom of the here and now that will give them joy and peace in the Holy Spirit!

Once we understand our three-part makeup, we are ready to proceed on to:

Re-Start Key Principle #2 – Go Inward to His Presence

Make sure that you engage in the activation and training exercises at the end of this chapter, regardless of where you are in your spiritual growth. Activation by practicing is the lifeline to your relationships with Father God, Christ Jesus and the Holy Spirit. Remember, most believers have the knowledge but fail to activate and train.

Activation Requires Training and Doing

I just heard the Holy Spirit say, *"You cannot be activated unless you train!"* People can lay hands on you and say, "You are now activated into this ministry, or that calling," but until you actually *train and do,* nothing will take place other than you are able to say that someone activated you into something.

These practice exercises can accelerate you quickly into the Kingdom of God and the supernatural realm of ruling and reigning in this present life. Access and entrance into the life of the Spirit and the walk toward maturity is the most exciting way to live this life.

Do *not* attempt to do all the exercises in a day! Take the first one and practice it every day until you no longer must look at the paper. *Commit it to memory*! Then proceed on to the next exercise. These activation and training exercises are a lifelong endeavor! Make them a daily, habitual lifestyle.

Practice does not make *perfect*! Practice makes *permanent*! So make your permanent perfect!

Activation and Training Exercise #1

Evaluating My Self (Soul)

(Read through all the instructions before you begin.)

Examine yourselves to see whether you are in the faith; test yourselves. Do you not realize that Christ Jesus is in you? (Emphasis added)

2 Corinthians 13:5 (NIV)

Take a moment right here and evaluate yourself. Write the answers down so you can really think about your Christian walk with the Lord. Evaluate yourself with these questions:

1. Am I growing in my walk with Christ? Or am I just attending church, doing a lot of "stuff" there, and calling it walking with Christ?
2. Do I still struggle with habits or negative actions and behavior that I can't seem to conquer and leave behind?
3. Are things in my past affecting my present life, which will affect my future life?
4. Do I now understand my three-part nature: spirit, soul, and body, and how the spirit should be the ruler of my life? Am I walking in the invisible Spirit?
5. Have I ever intentionally trained myself to go inward to the Presence of the Lord? Have I made that connection with Him and has it become habitual?
6. Do I carry His Presence with me to the extent that I am aware of Him with me on the path of life?

Do not go any further until you have asked yourself these important questions! It is not too late to have a *Re-Start*, or a do-over! Just as a reminder:

"Re-Start"[14] is defined as the following:

- To start anew.
- To resume (something, such as an activity) after interruption.
- To resume operation.

"Principle"[15] is defined as the following:

- A moral rule or belief that helps you know what is right and wrong and that influences your actions.
- A rule or code of conduct.
- A law or fact of nature that explains how something works or why something happens.

Follow the Activation and Training Exercises to *Re-Start* this code of conduct so that you may get it fully into your daily life.

---

[14] *https://www.merriam-webster.com/dictionary/restart*
[15] *https://www.merriam-webster.com/dictionary/principle*

Activation and Training Exercise #2

Changing My Mindset!

(Train for at least 15 minutes each day in a quiet place.)

1. Memorize and repeat the following on a daily basis:
   - My foot is on the Rock and my mind is made up! Following Jesus is my choice, not an option. I refuse to allow any person, place, or thing to abort my destiny and purpose in following Christ Jesus!
   - I am a spirit who operates a spiritual realm, who possesses, seizes, and takes control of my soul (my mind, will, reasoning, and emotions) and lives in a body—a house for the Lord!

2. Memorize and write your own positive daily declarations and use them every day. (Example)
   - I can do all things through Christ who strengthens me. (Philippians 4:13)
   - I am more than a conqueror. (Romans 8:37)
   - Jesus is my rock and my salvation. Whom shall I fear? (Psalm 27:1)
   - No weapon formed against me shall prosper. (Isaiah 54:17)
   - By His stripes I am healed. (Emphasis added) (Isaiah 53:5)

Activation and Training Exercise #3

Decree and Confession Refusals

(Read through all the instructions before you begin.)

Oxford Dictionary defines a *decree* as "an official order issued by a legal authority." As a believer, you have been given power and authority to drive out demons and to cure diseases. (Luke 9:1)

Making a confession out loud, as an official order issued by a legal authority, orders your day right! The Bible says you have the power of *"life and death in your tongue."* (Proverbs 18:21) What comes out of your mouth is important.

Write the following decrees on 3" x 5" index cards and carry them with you. Practice saying them aloud with vim and vigor, aggressively. You are issuing an official legal order to the spirit world. You are planning your steps as ordered by the Lord. (Proverbs 20:24)

SAY OUT LOUD! Create your own note cards and repeat every day or as needed!

Decree #1 Confession Refusals

- I refuse to speak ungodly words.
- I refuse to listen to gossip from others
- I refuse to let materialism lead my life.
- I refuse to walk in fear and intimidation

Decree #2 Confession Refusals

- I refuse to allow my mind, my will, and my emotions to keep me in unforgiveness.
- I refuse to argue in my mind.
- I refuse to live in captivity.
- I refuse to allow other people's words and actions to beat me down.

Decree #3 Confession Refusals

- I refuse to make excuses and justify bad behavior.
- I refuse to allow other people's judgments to affect my self-esteem.
- I refuse to perceive difficulties as problems. I can do all things through Christ. (Philippians 4:13)
- I refuse to surround myself with negative people.

(Close each decree with the following statement aloud.)

And I do this by the delegated authority and power given to me by the powerful, wonderful, and majestic name of Jesus Christ!

Now, write out your own decrees and confessions! Keep decreeing these confessions until you see results and then write out a new set. Don't forget to end with the above statement.

Decree and Confession Refusals

I Refuse _____.

I Refuse _____.

I Refuse _____.

I Refuse _____.

I Refuse _____.

I Refuse _____.

I Refuse _____.

I Refuse _____.

Activation and Training Exercise #4

WHY MEMORIZE THE SCRIPTURES?

1. Jesus memorized the Scriptures. He quoted twenty-four books of the Old Testament almost 180 times in the New Testament. If it was important enough for Jesus, then it is important enough for me.

2. You can't apply or teach something you don't have in your heart! The Old Testament exhorts us, in Deuteronomy 6:4-9, to *"bind God's law on our foreheads, teach it to our children, talk about it wherever we go, and make it a part of our life."* (Emphasis added)

   • King David says, *"I have hidden your word in my heart that I might not sin against you."* (Psalm 119:11)

   • To keep it simple: No word in; no word out! When you don't have your Bible with you, your spirit will remind you of the Word that lives in you, so you can make the right decisions and choices.

3. Renew Your Mind! When you have stinking thinking, changing the thoughts inside your head will change your attitude toward those circumstances. 2 Corinthians 10:5 says that we have a responsibility to *"take every thought captive to obey Christ."* (ESV)

   • Romans 12:2 NLT says this best: *"Don't copy the behavior and customs of this world, but let God transform you into a new person by changing the way you think. Then you will learn to know God's will for you, which is good and pleasing and perfect."*

Important First Scriptures!

(Make it personal by inserting personal pronouns.)

Scripture Memorization

For as he thinks in his heart, so is he.

Proverbs 23:7 (NKJV)

Confession: *For as I think in my heart, so am I.*

*****

We are more than conquerors through Him who loved us.

Romans 8:37 (NKJV)

Confession: *I am more than a conqueror through Him who loved me.*

*****

For though we walk in the flesh, we do not war according to the flesh. ⁴For the weapons of our warfare are not carnal but mighty in God for pulling down strongholds, ⁵casting down arguments and every high thing that exalts itself against the knowledge of God, bringing every thought into captivity to the obedience of Christ,

2 Corinthians 10:3-5 (NKJV)

Confession: *For though I walk in the flesh, I do not war according to the flesh. For the weapons of my warfare are not carnal [soulish, fleshly] but mighty in God for pulling down strongholds, [in my mind, will, emotions] casting down arguments [thoughts, reasonings] and every high [proud] thing that exalts itself against the knowledge of God, bringing every thought into captivity to the obedience of Christ.* (Emphasis added)

Find Scriptures that speak to your heart! There are sixty-six books of the Bible from which to choose.

7

<u>GO INWARD TO HIS PRESENCE</u>

*To them God willed to make known what are the
riches of the glory of this mystery among the
Gentiles: which is Christ in you, the hope of glory.*

Colossians 1:27 (NKJV)

*Therefore we do not lose heart. Even though our
outward man is perishing, yet the inward man is
being renewed day by day.*

2 Corinthians 4:16 (NKJV)

In the last chapter, we received the understanding that:

*I am a spirit who operates a spiritual realm, who
possesses, seizes, and takes control of my soul,
my mind, will, reasoning, emotions, and lives in a
body.*

The question then is "How does all of this work together?"

In order to hear the voice of God, you must first know how
to make a connection with God! It would be impossible to reach
the world wide web if you are not connected by Wi-Fi,
computer, phone, or some other device. God requires a
connection before He will speak to you! He wants to talk to you
personally and individually. He always wants to have a
conversation with you because He loves you and created you.

A man's spirit is the part of him that *knows* God! This means
that you are in the same class with God because God is Spirit.
(John 4:24) Those who come to Him, also worship Him (talk to
Him) by their spirit. God is Spirit. We are now spirit by means of

45

the salvation experience. (John 3:16-17) We cannot touch God physically because we are spirit. The way to communicate to God is through our *Re-lifed spirit*.

Now let me ask you a few questions. Where is God? Where is Jesus? Where is the Holy Spirit? Yes, they are in heaven, but they are also *in us*, in our *inner man*, our *new-lifed spirit*!

We can't see them, but they are there never the less! The word says:

> But if the Spirit of Him who raised Jesus from the dead dwells IN YOU, He who raised Christ from the dead will also give life to your mortal bodies through His Spirit who dwells IN YOU. (Emphasis added)
>
> Romans 8:11 (NKJV)

This is how it worked before the Fall. God would move upon man's spirit. Man's spirit would move upon his *soul* (mind, will, emotions), and his *soul* would get into agreement with the newly created *spirit*. The *soul* would direct the *body* and actions and behaviors would follow.

The simple understanding is

1. The spirit serves God.
2. The soul serves the spirit.
3. The body serves the soul.

Through the rebellion of Adam and Eve, the spirit was set aside and the soul took control of man. Now, instead of the spirit serving God, the soul began to serve itself—its desires, wants, and passions. (James 1:14)

After your conversion, your own human spirit, which is deep within your innermost being, is touched by God and is made alive and functioning. Conversion is not just a matter of turning from sin. There is also a turning from outward things to the innermost part of your being—to the place where the Lord has come to reside.

Your spirit (inner man) will then invite your soul (mind, will, emotions) to re-direct from its business of the moment and instead will prompt you to turn inward to the center of your being where God resides. This is not a hard thing. When you turn to God inwardly, it becomes easier and easier to return there again and again. Remember, God the Father, Jesus the Son, and the Holy Spirit reside in you now!

As your soul turns inward—as it yields to that inner voice or prompting—the spirit can then speak to the soul and the soul will obey what the spirit is instructing it to do.

A trade will occur. This is what you want your soul to do. The spirit will trade you peace for unrest, joy for sorrow, and the garment of praise where there is a burden, heaviness, or depression in your soul. (Isaiah 61:3) When your mind is tormented with worry, trying to figure things out, the Spirit of God can't trade your unrest for his peace. You must take control of all thinking, and surrender it, yielding to God inwardly. If your soul is not focused, it will jump quickly from one thought to another. This shows restlessness and lack of inner peace.

The more you turn inward to your spirit where God is located, the nearer you are drawn to Him.

Moving into that innermost place with God, again and again, will establish you so firmly that it will become natural, even habitual, to live in the presence of God.

In order to succeed, you must withdraw from your emotional state, situations, troubles, health problems, etc. Take control of rambling, negative thoughts. You can do this. It is in God's DNA flowing in you. Simply yield your soul to Christ who lives in the center of you.

Activation and Training Exercise #1

Right now, bow your head to your heart! Take a few deep breaths—breathe in and out for a few times. Quiet your thoughts and worries. Now, release all the strain and stress by whispering the name of Jesus. See what that did for you?

Learning to go inward by putting to silence every thought, and focusing on Christ will ensure that everything inside of your soul will move to quietness, stillness, and peace with God (2 Corinthians. 10:5)

No other rules, no more Step 1, Step 2...just this one simple movement.

> *The soul must do this one thing:*
> *Turn inward to the God inside.*

The Spirit will then send the breath of the Holy Spirit to your soul that you may *"walk in the Spirit and not fulfill the lusts of the flesh."* (Galatians. 5:16 Emphasis added) He will purify your soul as He continues to draw you inward.

Connection is the Goal!

- The soul, (mind, will, and emotions) will become purified as the Lord Himself takes gradual possession of your life. You will begin to look more like Jesus.
- It is in this place that He will begin to lead you into a deep relationship of love and begin to manifest Himself to you as the Lord of all.

You are now connected with God! Practice until you can make a connection within seconds.

Now that you are connected, let us move to the purpose of being connected. Don't get alarmed! I haven't forgotten about how to hear God's voice consistently.

The Soul and Sub-Conscious Memory

The soul has within it the subconscious memory where everything that has ever happened in a person's life, good or bad, is permanently stored. The sub-conscious mind is like a huge memory bank. Its job is to store and retrieve data. It doesn't think or reason. All your habits and behavior are stored there. It is said by some that by the time you reach the age of 21, you have already permanently stored more than one hundred times the contents of the entire *Encyclopedia Britannica*.

My husband was told as a young boy, "You aren't worth the salt in the cornbread." That affected everything in his life. He decided that he would prove that statement to be a lie. He was worth the salt in his cornbread! Someone else, however, could have allowed that memory to affect them in a negative way.

Others have suffered great trauma through physical or mental abuse. Pain, fear, and everything about the trauma was recorded in their sub-conscious memory. If they were told as a child, "Don't touch that stove, it will burn you," but they touched it anyway, the pain of that experience is in their subconscious memory.

You have heard the expression "I'm a Soulman." A *soulman* is described as a person who is ruled or controlled by their human nature (soul) instead of their God nature (spirit). Some call it the flesh.

If your human nature was strong enough for you to handle life, then you would not need a Savior, Healer, and Deliverer! Being a strong person will not conquer the weakness of your outer life. I am not saying that it doesn't help to have a strong constitution. You can change some things about yourself with your own human strength. However, trauma, deep-seated fears, and habits, can only be traded, and replaced with new memories by the power of the Holy Spirit within you!

Outward change and improvement will begin to take place. Remember, trading takes place. God is removing old pains, hurts, and heartaches embedded in your subconscious memories which still control you.

Habits will change and some will begin to leave. Depression must go! Suicide has no power! Those bad memories will be replaced with the truth of what Christ has to say about you .

> *Outward change and improvements are totally dependent on going inward to His presence!*

When we receive Christ, He cleanses us from all our sins and wipes the slate clean. Now the newly created, *Re-lifed* spirit inside of us has the job of dealing with the soul, where all those negative words, pain, trauma, habits, and things from our past are recorded and stored.

One of my favorite expressions to say is, "Jesus comes into us to save our soul (mind, will, and emotions)."

He wants to give us new memories—good ones. (1 Corinthians 15:44-46; Galatians 5; Romans 8; Matthew 16:24-26)

One day the Holy Spirit gave me an example of this by showing me a picture of prayer. It blew my socks off. Our God has made this human body and the inner man so great.

Activation and Training Exercise #2

Visualization Exercise

How to yield and surrender your soul.

- Picture yourself bowing your head to your chest in prayer.
- The Spirit is within you (your chest).
- Your soul is in your head (mind, thoughts, will, choices, emotions, feelings).

As you quiet all that stinking thinking and unrest, just begin to say the name of Jesus. Keep doing this until you sense His peace.

This is a good picture of a yielded, surrendered soul, mind, will, and emotions to the spirit. Now the spirit can begin to help you not just *talk the talk* but *walk the walk*! (Galatians 5:16-17)

Taking this simple first step is key to being able to make your connection with God!

Many years ago, a dear friend traveled with me to get away for a few days. The time was to be spent in seeking the face of the Lord, hearing from Him and resting. Little did I know that all the activations and training at this time spent with the Lord would be a part of the writing of this book. Back to the story!

As we traveled to our destination, she was explaining to me how difficult it was for her to sense His presence and to hear the voice of God. Sometimes she felt that He was far away.

My friend had been a believer for many years but still struggled. Why did she struggle? Because she was not activated and trained at yielding up her mind, will and emotions to God in the beginning of her walk at her conversion. She did not know that she was a three-part being, so therefore she had no clue as

51

to how to submit her soul to her spirit, which was within her being.

Yes, for those of you asking the question, "Is this possible?" It is possible! He longs for you to be in His presence!

I heard myself say, "Let's try an experiment." My hand reached to turn on a worship CD as we traveled down the road. Our goal was to see how fast we could sense His presence in the car. She was to close her eyes and listen to the movement which took her attention off all the noise in her head. Then she was to whisper the name of Jesus.

Within a minute, His presence surrounded us. Within another 30 seconds, the presence of the Holy Spirit had filled the car and she joined me in worshipping and praising God, which we did for a period of time.

After the time of worshipping, she said, "How did you do that? I felt Him all around us! It was so quick! You could see Him on you and His presence filled the car and moved over me. How do I cultivate that on a continuous basis? You are driving down the road! How could you bring His presence so powerfully while watching the traffic, slowing and speeding up? I want His *presence* in my life this way!"

This simple expression of yielding to Him and focusing on Him brought His *presence*. Please know that it was not magic.

My life had been spent learning how to connect with Jesus. You can experience His presence all the time as well! Practice, practice, practice these activations! You will not be disappointed.

> *For what man knows the things of a man except the spirit of the man which is <u>in him</u>? Even so <u>no one knows the things of God except the Spirit of God</u>.* (Emphasis added)
>
> 1 Corinthians 2:11 (NKJV)

Look at the underlined portion of 1 Corinthians 2:11. The spirit of man in you has been made alive and is now the place where God speaks to you and helps you navigate through this life in the world system.

The power of the gospel is transformation! We get to change, trading our old man for a new man.

> That you <u>put off</u>, concerning your former conduct, the old man which grows corrupt according to the deceitful lusts, [23]and <u>be renewed</u> in the <u>spirit [soul] of your mind</u>, [24]and that you <u>put on</u> the <u>new man</u> which <u>was created according to God, in true righteousness and holiness</u>. (Emphasis added)
>
> Ephesians 4:22-24 (NKJV)

Your spirit has come to change the things recorded in your soul through the process of healing and deliverance. Halleluiah!

Remember: This is not hearing-only Christianity!

The entire purpose of this book is to get you to realize that there is something, you as a believer must do besides hearing and sitting in church. Being a believer is more than participating in activities at church!

Just think how different society would be if Christian believers activated and practiced the trading principle. (Ephesians 4:20-24)

Salvation is the Greek word *Sozo*. Defined, it means not only salvation but: *healed, healing, recover, save, saving, whole, wholly, wholesome*.[16] In short, saved, healed and delivered. *WooHoo!*

When you were converted to Christ, you received

---

[16] *Strong's Talking Greek-Hebrew Dictionary, Gk 4982*

everything you needed in Christ, in your new *Re-lifed* spirit, to totally and completely walk as Jesus walked.

Emotions and feelings can be charged with anxiety, anger, unforgiveness, etc. The *Re-Start* key principle of going inward to His presence will allow God to deal with these emotions and bring the emotions to a peaceful and restful state of mind.

Whatever you focus on in your mind (soul, your human-ness) will bring two results:

1) More agitation, unrest, worry, stress, bitterness,
2) A trade for peace, forgiveness, love, etc.

This inward turn toward the center of God inside of you is the solid foundation of all spiritual progress.

> *You can't begin to hear accurately from God on a consistent basis, until you learn how to take control of your un-yielded and un-surrendered soul and make a connection with God!*

A few years ago, the Holy Spirit gave me inspiration to write a song about the process of yielding to the Spirit.

Yielded, Holy Spirit[17]

Yielded, Holy Spirit!
Be Exalted on My Throne! (Spirit)[18]
My Soul Yields, Holy Spirit! Yielded and United,
To You Alone! (Going Inward to His Presence)
If my Soul is Ruling on the Throne, Lord

---

[17] *Words & Music Written By: Lou Ellen Hoffman, © PAu-3-428-779 Aug 26, 2009*
[18] *() Inserted for clarity Not part of the song*

Then Your Holy Spirit is Still
I Yield My Mind, my Will, and my Emotions, (Soul)
To Deep Workings of Your Will (Spirit)
When my Soul gets Quiet and Rested,
Then the Holy Spirit Reveals The Truth
To my Mind, Will, and Emotions
To the Glory of His Will.

There is another old gospel chorus that comes to mind which wonderfully describes what happens when you learn to go inward to His presence: "Jesus, on the inside, working on the outside. O, what a change in my life."[19]

An outward transformation will begin to happen which others will be able to see. As God becomes stronger within you, others will be pulled or drawn to get to know you. They won't necessarily understand it. There will just be something about you that causes them to want to have the joy and peace they see in your life! Of course, that drawing is to the God *in you!*

And I, if I am lifted up from the earth, will draw all peoples to Myself.

John 12:32 (NKJV)

If you attempt to deal with all the issues of life by yourself, you will feel defeated and discouraged. As a Pastor, I have personally seen so much of this defeated behavior in the Body of Christ. Believers have no joy, no peace, no victory in their lives. They are zombies—just doing what they have always done, following the religious crowd who are stuck in their rituals and dead services! This is simply because we have missed activating and training and using these powerful *Re-Start Principles* at the beginning of our walk instead of thirty or forty years later.

---

[19] *Carol Cymbala © 1988 Word Music, LLC (a div. of Word Music Group, Inc.) Carol Joy Music (Main) (Admin by Clearbox Rights, LLC)*

A Progression!

There is a progression in going inward to His presence.

Think about the growth of a baby. At birth, it is so important for the baby to make a connection with its parents. Eating, diaper changes, and sleeping is an important part of its growth. Getting familiar with the atmospheres and the new sounds around it takes a period of adjustment.

What would happen if the baby never learned to smile, laugh, roll over, crawl, and walk? That's right! The baby's body would grow large, but who has ever seen a parent carrying around a grown adult body?

The believer's progressive walk is similar to that of a baby's. First, we must learn to go inward so that the outward actions and behaviors of our human-ness, our soul, will change and develop. It is this outward change that bears witness that we are *"sons and daughters of the Most High God."* (2 Corinthians 6:8) We and others can see what God is doing outwardly!

Secondly, we must progress onward toward the things that are spiritual.

> *For our light affliction, which is but for a moment, is working for us a far more exceeding and eternal weight of glory,* ¹⁸ *while we <u>do not look at</u> the <u>things</u> which are <u>seen, but at the things</u> which are <u>not seen</u>. For the <u>things</u> which are <u>seen are temporary</u>, but the <u>things</u> which <u>are not seen are eternal</u>.* (Emphasis added)

2 Corinthians 4:17-18 (NKJV)

Did you read the underlined scripture? Say it out loud! Here, let me help you....

"Do not look at things seen.... but at the things not seen. Things seen are temporary! Things not seen are eternal!"

Our walk with Christ begins with us seeing the seen (visible) realm,[20] and not seeing the unseen (invisible) realm. To progress properly in our walk with the Lord at salvation, we must leave the realm of the seen (visible) realm and begin to be introduced to the unseen (invisible) realm, where we live by *faith* and not by *sight*. (2 Corinthians 5:7)

Going to church is important, and getting involved in activities and events are important but that is not spiritual growth. True spiritual growth and faith come from the invisible Kingdom of God!

Are you beginning to catch a glimpse of why some have a defeated state of mind? There is so much more to going inward to His presence. It would take another book or more to describe it!

Start your activation and training now!

---

[20] *Realm is defined as a "Kingdom."*

Activation and Training Exercise
How to Go Inward to His Presence

(Read through all the instructions before you begin.)

1. Find a place where you can be alone and undisturbed. Make it a quiet place.

2. Turn on quiet and passionate worship music! Stop the music if you find your mind going to the music and staying there, or if you begin to hum or sing along in your head. It has become a distraction! The purpose is to help you focus on Him.

3. Close your eyes and take a few calm deep breaths. Relax your body.

4. Think about your relationship with your heavenly Father.

5. Choose an inspiring word or a simple phrase and repeat it silently in your mind. Example:
   - I love You, Father!
   - You are my God, my King, my Lord.
   - I desire to make a connection with You.
   - I want to come into Your presence!

You may choose to say the name of Jesus silently in your mind.

6. Pause and wait for His peace to begin to fill your being. This is a sign that you are connected.

7. Be persistent and consistent with this exercise. Do not give up! It may require some repenting of sins as they come to mind. (See How to Cleanse Your Soul Sub-Conscious: The Process)
   You will know when you make a connection when your mind becomes quiet and still, and there are no longer any troubled thoughts of your situations, or circumstances.

Activation and Training Exercise
Forgiveness Soul Cleaning Exercise

(Read through all the instructions before you begin.)

Please Get Your Bible and Read: Matthew 18:23-35

This is the life lesson of holding things in your heart such as resentment, bitterness, and unforgiveness. This life lesson instructs us that if we do not forgive those who have hurt us, we get turned over to the torturers. Now, I don't know about you, but that is certainly not something a person would want to happen.

1. Make a list of names
   - To begin forgiving others, write down the name of every person (even if they are no longer living) who has irritated or offended you in some way. If the hurt or upset is still with you, their name goes on the list.
   - You will be amazed at the memories that come to you. People may come to your mind that you haven't thought about in years.
   - Ask God to bring to mind those you need to forgive. As He reveals them, write their names in the space provided.
   - Briefly describe what or why you need to forgive.
   - As you make your list, be sure to include family members, authority figures, and strangers who caused you pain.
   - Remember also church(es), business associates, doctors, schoolteachers, boyfriends, and girlfriends you need to forgive.
   - Remember to forgive *yourself* for any wrongs you are holding against yourself.
   - Don't show your list to anyone.
2. Ask Father God to forgive *you* for holding unforgiveness in your heart.

Sample Prayer

"Father God I ask You to forgive me for the sin of holding unforgiveness against the people on my list. (You may name them individually if you feel the need.) Your Word declares that if I do not forgive others their sins, You will not forgive me of my sins. (Matthew 6:15) Cleanse me and now help me as I spend this time releasing those who have sinned against me by word, action, or deed. Thank You for Your love and forgiveness, in Jesus Name. Amen!

3. Spend some time forgiving each person on your list (See 4 to proceed in this.)
   - Now, forgive!
   - Forgiving each person is a *choice* you must make.
   - Forgiveness doesn't depend on others.
   - It is not necessary to *ask* others for forgiveness.

If they have not *asked* to be forgiven, it is not usually necessary to talk to them and *tell* them you forgive them. Forgiveness is a *choice* you make before God.

Once you say the affirmation, feel the truth of the words in your body. Notice how good it feels to let go. Continue to do this with each person on your list.

4. Look at the first name on your list, close your eyes, hold the image of that person in your mind, and tell them:

"I forgive you and release you. I hold back no unforgiveness. My forgiveness for you is total. I am free and you are free."

   - I give up my right to *think* about you.
   - I give up my right to *speak* about you.
   - I give up my right to *vindicate* myself.
   - I give up my right to seek *retaliation*.

"I fully and freely release you and set you free for the Lord to deal with in His Grace. By the grace I have found in Jesus, I now declare you to be forgiven."

(Continue until you have made this declaration over every person on your list)

NOTE: This exercise must be used daily to ensure that you are not holding unforgiveness in your heart. One of the greatest tools of satan in the Body of Christ is the spirit of offense. He has entered the doors of our houses of worship and tricked God's people into thinking that we have a right to *defend or justify* our actions and behaviors toward our brothers and our sisters.

Unforgiveness is rampant in local church fellowships. Come on now. Give that statement an Amen! You know this is true. Our position should be to "turn the other cheek." This is genuine forgiveness. (Mark 11:25; Ephesians 4:32; 1 John 1:9-10; Matthew 18:21-22; James 5:16; Luke 6:27; Colossians 3:13)

Sample Offenses: (These are real live statements)

- They didn't shake my hand!
- Arguing over the carpet, etc.
- I've been here the longest, but they are the ones that get all the credit.
- I should have that position.
- He ignored me and didn't speak to me!
- They hurt my feelings!
- I don't feel like I belong!

Activation and Training Exercise
How to Cleanse Your Soul (sub-conscious)
Process Visualization Exercise

(Read through all the instructions before you begin.)

The soul and the subconscious memory can get clean as the Lord takes gradual possession. Trading takes place!

1. Visualize your soul inside your head including the subconscious memory.
2. See all the things that have happened in your life stored there as black dots. Can you see that?
3. Now see a great bright light shining on one of those dots. Maybe God shows you that the dot is pride in your heart.
4. Confess what the Lord shows you as sin.

Example: *"Father I see that I am holding pride in my heart and thinking too highly of myself. I ask for cleaning right now."*

5. Watch it as it totally disappears right before your eyes.
6. Do this on a regular daily or weekly basis. The more you make your God connection, the faster your life will begin to change!
7. The Holy Spirit is the light that comes to shine on something inside of your soul that needs cleansing. This is a gradual process in our walk with the Lord. The reason it is a process is that only our spirit was *Re-lifed* and transformed. Our soul is in the process of being renewed daily. (James 1:21; 1 Thessalonians 5:23)
8. This visualization exercise is one to use every time the Holy Spirit brings conviction to you about an action, thought, or behavior.
9. Learn it Now! This will become one of the spiritual tools to help you grow consistently, properly, and advance into the Kingdom of God in the supernatural!

Activation and Training Exercise
Meditate the Scriptures?

This Book of the Law shall not depart from your mouth, but you shall meditate in it day and night, that you may observe to do according to all that is written in it. For then you will make your way prosperous, and then you will have good success.

Joshua 1:8 (NKJV)

God wants to restore meditation to the Body of Christ! The enemy of our soul knows if he can keep us upset and confused, he can gain an open door into our lives. One definition of *meditate* means *"to engage in contemplation or reflection"*[21]. Another says it is to *"engage in focused thought on scriptural passages or mysteries of a religion, especially Christianity."*[22]

Another pattern of thought is to *"ruminate."*[23]

The word *ruminate* means to *"go over in the mind repeatedly and often casually or slowly; to chew repeatedly for an extended period."*

My absolute favorite meaning of this word is to *chew again what has been chewed slightly* and *swallowed*: *chew the cud*. Yes, like a cow. They chew it and chew it and then regurgitate or ruminate it back up and chew some more.

The purpose of meditation is to help our minds stay free from worries and mental discomfort by meditating on God's Word. You will experience the *joy of the Lord* in a continuous manner and will learn how to stay peaceful amid trouble.

---

[21] *www.merriam-webster.com/dictionary/meditate*
[22] *www.thefreedictionary.com/meditate*
[23] *www.merriam-webster.com/dictionary/ruminate*

You [Father God] will keep him [me] in perfect peace, whose mind is stayed on You, [Father God] (Emphasis added)

Isaiah 26:3 (NKJV)

Meditation is about yielding and surrendering our thoughts to the Spirit of God within us!

(Before you begin, read all instructions.)

1. Find a comfortable place! Sit with your eyes closed. Be silent!
2. Take some deep breaths slowly and release all the tension, etc.
3. Quite all thoughts and distractions in the soul (mind).
4. Silently use the name of Jesus if you are having difficulty with your thoughts.
5. Once you are focused, read the scripture above, Isaiah 26:3 (NKJV).
6. Begin to say silently, in your head, the first line of the scripture passage. Personalize it by adding personal pronouns or even your name: *Father God will keep 'Lou' in perfect peace* (added my own name for clarity).
7. Begin to visualize what *perfect peace* means to you, maybe a picture of Jesus holding you in His arms, picture yourself in whatever way you remember being at peace and rest. Stay here until you can visualize yourself in peace. (See next exercise - Meditation Visualization.)
8. The Holy Spirit may speak something to your heart a phrase or a word. When He does, acknowledge it with a thought, "Thank you Holy Spirit" and write it down.
9. Take the next phrase when you are ready! *"Whose mind is stayed on Father God."*

10. Visualize a picture of your head. Inside is your soul, composed of thoughts. (See Chapter 8: Activation and Training Exercise: How to Yield, Surrender Your Soul!").

11. Picture God's word's in your mind such as peace, joy, love, or any other that the Holy Spirit speaks to you!

12. You will discover that after meditation your mind is clear and all confusion is gone. Cobwebs and distractions have vanished!

Activation and Training Exercise
Meditation Visualization

(Read through all the instructions before you begin.)

Close your eyes and use the first phrase. Think about it!

Visualize seeing and doing what it says.

Do not proceed to the next one until you have sufficiently visualized it.

1. The *fear* of the Lord is to hate evil. (Proverbs 8:13)
2. While we live, we live to please the Lord. (Romans. 14:8)
3. We will *prosper* and be in *health* as our *soul*, (mind, will, and emotions), prospers. (3 John 1:2)
4. I am identified by what I am wearing! (Ephesians 4:2 NKJV)
5. The *grace* of God will *perfect*, *confirm* and *establish me*. (See 1 Peter 5:10 NKJV)

You may add more as you begin to visualize these.

My sheep hear my voice, and I know them, and they follow me. (Emphasis added)

John 10:27 (KJV)

He who belongs to God hears what God says. (Emphasis added)

John 8:47a (NIV)

8

<u>Hearing and Recognizing the Three Voices</u>

How effective would you be if you went into a service or attended a class every week and listened to what the instructor was telling you to do, but you never put it into *practice*? The answer: Not very effective and not very skilled at the task. It is the same principle for hearing God's Voice and all the other principles in the Word of God.

How effective would you be if you never practiced your trade or hands-on experience? This is one of the reasons we have vocational schools across the nations.

It is important for us to have knowledge, and knowledge is key to growing and operating in the Kingdom of God, but not just head knowledge. It must be heart knowledge.

> *Knowledge only without practical experience could get you fired on a job!*

There are a couple of men in our local fellowship who work for the oil industry. Do you think they could do their jobs with knowledge only? What about operating a barge or moving a rig without practice? How about an electrician with no practical experience; a carpenter; a professional dancer? The answer again is you would not make a very good employee, worker, electrician, carpenter, professional dancer, or pianist, if you only knew how to read or receive the instructions but not actually engage and do the instructions.

Yet we attempt to live our lives for Christ without practicing the manual (*Bible Code of Conduct Manual*) that we have been given.

Week after week, we attend conferences, weekly fellowships, and special revival services with a *"hearing only"* mindset. This is what *religion* has trained us to do. It is called: *"having a form of godliness but denying its power."* (2 Timothy 3:5 NKJV Emphasis added) A form of Godliness is doing a thing by rote and routine with no joy, peace, or growth.

Practice Is Key to Hearing the Voice of God

Here are a few scriptures to present this concept of practicing the *code of conduct book*—the Bible:

> *The things which you learned and received and heard and saw in me, these do, [practice] and the God of peace will be with you.* (Emphasis added)
>
> Philippians 4:9 (NKJV)

> *Be diligent to present yourself approved to God, a worker [someone who practices his trade] who does not need to be ashamed, rightly dividing the word of truth.* (Emphasis added)
>
> 2 Timothy 2:15 (NKJV)

Yes, we are going to repeat the phrase again:

"P*ractice is the key to hearing the voice of God.*"

This book will not help you at all if you don't take the *Activations and Training Exercises* and begin to make them a daily and weekly part of your walk as a believer. Instead, it will just become another book (a form of godliness) you have read, with no real change in your walk with Christ.

Is God Speaking to Me?

Someone has said, *"God is always speaking to us!"* Why are we not hearing His voice? Why are believers who have served the Lord for years, not perceiving when He is speaking to them?

I remember being saved at an early age as a kid. Hearing God speak to me was no problem at that time. It seemed as if He and I were communicating all the time. As the years flew by, however, I began to recognize that I was not hearing His voice as often.

One of the questions I pondered for years was, "God, why do I hear Your voice sometimes and then struggle to hear it at others?"

Hearing His voice and none other can sometimes confuse you if you haven't been *trained* to know His voice.

I can hear the Lord say, *"My sheep (children) who have spent time with Me all know My voice unquestionably." They are acquainted with My soft loving voice, My stern, no-nonsense voice and the many other voices spoken, just as a child knows its mom and dad's voice. When they hear those distinct voices, there is absolutely no question in My sheep's (children) mind that it is Me speaking to them. My sheep (children) can even hear My voice in a crowd of people. They know My voice that well."*

Our children also talk to us every day even as adults with children of their own. Sometimes it is several times a day. It is not necessary for them to tell us their name, or even that they are one of our kids. They call to see how we are doing, and to share something that they have heard or experienced in the day with their children. We could not imagine a day going by without communicating with our children.

Here is the big question. Do you believe our heavenly Father wants us to know His voice this well? Or, has He just saved us and left us as orphans in the world to never know when our daddy God speaks to us?

I believe that we all know the answer to this question. He wants to communicate with us as a father to sons and daughters. (John 8:47a)

Unfortunately, the body of believers in Christ still struggles with hearing His voice on a consistent basis. Some Christians believe that pastors, evangelists, or ministers are the only ones who hear the voice of God. Rubbish! Please don't be taken in by this lie from satan. (John 10:27)

The Solution to this Problem!

Pastors, special speakers, conferences and books have taught us educationally and scripturally regarding the need to hear the voice of God. They have also taught us the ways that God speaks to us, but we have not received any hands-on training in this area. Without practical application, we question and get confused over who is speaking to us.

Religion has trained us to come to church and listen to what the pastor is speaking.

The words of the old hymn, *"In the Garden,"* written by C. August Miles, (Public Domain), resonate with the truth that God wants to speak to us.

> *"I come to the garden alone,*
> *While the dew is still on the roses*
> *And the voice I hear, falling on my ear*
> *The Son of God discloses;*
> *[to make known something]*[24]
> *And He walks with me and He talks with me*

---

[24] *[] definition inserted*

And He tells me I am His own
And the joy we share as we tarry there
None other has ever known."

Disciples, believers, and Christians of Christ Jesus should expect to hear God's voice! Progression in the Kingdom of God and into the walk of the supernatural is central to all of life. (Matthew 6:9-13)

Hearing His voice opens the door (portal, gate) to minister to others! Hearing His voice opens the door (portal, gate) to the gifts of the Spirit! Hearing His voice opens the door (portal, gate) to the prophetic! Hearing His voice gives direction for our life!

Settle it in your heart today! God wants you to hear His voice more than you want to hear Him. His promise is that His sheep (all believers) will hear His voice. Over and over in the Word of God from Genesis to Revelation, we see the words, *"and God said."* Jesus, on many occasions, would speak out, *"He who has ears to hear, let him hear."* (Matthew 11:15; Mark 4:9, 19, 23)

He wants to talk with you! Your relationship with Him is important. He longs for you to put your relationship with Him as a priority. In my understanding, *first* was considered the highest priority! You have a choice to make. Do you keep bumbling along hoping you are hearing God's voice correctly? Or do you need a *Re-Start*, a *do-over,* and learn how to practice hearing His voice now?

Stop and pray this prayer with me! I sense the Holy Spirit prompting some of you, those of you who are so tired and weary from the struggle of trying to figure this God thing out by yourselves, so pray right now!

Heavenly Father! I want to hear Your voice and no other will I follow. Take me right where I am, in my walk with You, and show me how to truly engage with You!

My heart's desire is to know Your voice so well that we communicate all the live-long-day together! Draw me closer and closer to You, the God of Glory, so that I may receive the instructions, corrections, and things of the Spirit more clearly.

I yield myself to You by moving inward to Your presence! (Chapter 8: Go Inward to His Presence)

Let me hear your voice! Teach me, Father. Amen!

> *But this is what I commanded them, saying, "Obey My voice, and I will be your God, and you shall be My people. And walk in all the ways that I have commanded you, that it may be well with you."*
>
> Jeremiah 7:23 (NKJV)

> *While it is said: "Today, if you will hear His voice, Do not harden your hearts as in the rebellion."*
>
> Hebrews 3:15 (NKJV)

> *Obedience is better than sacrifice.*
>
> 1 Samuel 15:22 NLT

Everyone will agree that as a believer we are to obey the voice of our Father. Knowing His voice and how He speaks to us is the key that will take us into new dimensions of *the Kingdom of God in the here and now! (not just a ticket to heaven)*

Today we are surrounded by many voices. Some of those voices will attempt to lead us astray from the Lord. It is our response to those voices that will determine our destiny.

What Keeps Us from Hearing God's Voice?

The *Re-Start Principle* Key#1 is the understanding that you are not just a human being. Actually, you are a three-part being: You are a spirit who operates within a spiritual realm, a spirit who possesses, seizes and takes control of your soul (your mind, will, reasoning, emotions) and lives in a body! You are a three-part being!

Your old nature (BC: Before Christ) is controlled or ruled by your soul (mind, will, emotions). Your new nature (AC: After Christ) is controlled or ruled by your spirit. The old nature is what will keep you from hearing the voice of God—specifically, in your mind!

The Bible explains it this way:

> *I say then: Walk in the Spirit, and you shall not fulfill the lust of the flesh. 17For the flesh lusts against the Spirit, and the Spirit against the flesh; and these are contrary to one another, so that you do not do the things that you wish.*

> Galatians 5:16-17 (NKJV)

Simply put, there is a war going on in your head. The old flesh man—your humanness—has an ongoing tendency to sin and rebel against God. (Galatians 5:19-26)

The new nature—your spirit—has everything you need to be victorious in this life packaged inside of it, everything to live and conquer in this war. Yet you have the old nature man, (your soul) to deal with regarding desire, sin, and temptation. It takes constant training and trading the old flesh man for the new spirit man. Remember that once you have trained and traded sufficiently enough it becomes a natural flow from your spirit man. By the way, whichever nature you feed the most will become the strongest!

> *The nature you feed the most will become the strongest!*

If you feed the new spirit man nature, *Christ in you*, it will grow strong while the old flesh man (soul) will grow weaker and will allow the Spirit to rule it. The more you feed your flesh, (your soul, the mind, will, and emotions), and are guided by whatever is already programmed in your sub-conscious memory, the stronger the desires toward sin will grow and your God nature, the *Re-lifed* spirit inside of you, will grow weaker!

This is a powerful truth!

My mother worked for a large school system and was the director of 25 cafeterias. She would say to me repeatedly, "Lou Ellen! You are what you eat!" Need I say any more?

Who Would You Rather Talk To?

Would you rather talk to someone who doesn't listen to you, and doesn't care enough to hear what you are saying? Or, would you rather speak to someone who is listening closely to every word you are speaking?

Think about this: God commands us to listen and to obey His voice.[25] His purpose is for you to enter into a relationship with Him, listen for His voice, and then do what He is telling you. Sometimes He just wants to see how our day is going! Sometimes He wants to shower His love on us. Other times, He wants to show us something inside of our sub-conscious that needs to be traded. (Love for hate, for example.)

---

[25] *Deuteronomy 13:4; 27:10; 1 Samuel 12:14; 2 Kings 18:12; Jeremiah 26:13; Joel 2:11; Mark 5:7; Acts 7:31; Hebrews 3:16; 2 Peter 1:19; James 1:14-15*

Which Voice are you Obeying?

Is it the voice of your own desires, what you want, when you want it, and how you want it that you are obeying? Is it the voice of the thoughts in your head (soul) or is it the voice of God and His Word implanted and coming from your *Re-lifed* spirit? Could it be the voices of people around you? Which voice is louder? Which voice do you obey?

The voice you listen to will determine what happens in your present life and how you will live in the future.

Three Voices That Speak?

Everyone hears voices! There are thoughts that come to our mind as we go about our daily life. Everyone understands that hearing voices can be attributed to mental health issues, but we are not alluding to a mental health condition. We spend a lot of time listening to ourselves talk inside of our heads. We ask ourselves questions internally, without speaking. We ponder things internally. We read books with our inner voice. A study I read recently in the *Medical News Today* said: "*The brain treats talking inside of our heads as essentially the same thing as talking out loud, according to new research published in the journal eLife...*"

My religious background was Pentecostal. Programmed into me was the belief that there were *two* internal voices that spoke to Christian believers. One was the voice of God! The other was the voice of satan. Anything that didn't sound like God or that was negative was the devil.

But things got very confusing when I tried to attribute all my inner thoughts to only God and satan.

It wasn't until many years later that I discovered, by experience and through study of the Word for myself, that there are three voices that speak to us as individuals.

Here was the process I learned to use to determine who was speaking internally.

Let's identify these internal voices. They can speak to every individual. They are:

1. The voice of God.
2. The voice of satan.
3. The voice of your own human-ness, the un-surrendered, un-yielded thoughts in your mind, (soul), your *flesh.*

There are two voices which speak into your carnal mind. One is your human voice. The second is satan's voice. God's voice does not speak to your head! He speaks from His *Re-lifed* spirit inside of you only when you have yielded and gone inward to Him. (*Chapter 8 Activation and Training Exercise*)

> But he who enters by the door is the shepherd of the sheep. ³To him the doorkeeper opens, and the sheep hear his voice; and he calls his own sheep by name and leads them out. ⁴And when he brings out his own sheep, he goes before them; and the sheep follow him, for they know his voice. ⁵Yet they will by no means follow a stranger, but will flee from him, for they do not know the voice of strangers."

John 10:2-5 (NKJV)

God is speaking to His sheep! Believers are called sheep! In this passage above, they learn to hear and recognize the voice of their shepherd. Once they know the voice of their shepherd, they will not respond to another shepherd if he calls to them. They will *not* follow another stranger's voice.

Jesus is saying that He has a voice which we can hear, and there is a stranger's voice we can also hear. Important truth! As sheep of His pasture, we must know when God is speaking to us. And just let me say, He is speaking to us way more than we are listening.

The Way God Speaks!

There are many ways that God can speak to you! One is through His Word, the Bible (2 Timothy 3:16; John 17:17). Have you ever been desperate, needing an answer, and began reading the Word? Maybe you just opened it up to a page and your eyes focused on a scripture that answered your worries or questions? (*By the way, this generally happens to newborn babies in Christ*)

His Word is a primary way He communicates His will with us—His desires, the moral codes He has laid out for us in a hands-on physical way.

He can speak to us through a vision or by a dream. He spoke to the Apostle Paul in this way in Acts 16:6-10. Using other people to speak into our hearts is yet another way. He can also speak to us through His Spirit who lives in us! (John 14:17; 1 Corinthians 3:16) This is referred to as the *inner voice*. (My brother, Donald Dees, has a wonderful book on Amazon on this very subject.[26])

These are all wonderful ways that we hear from God, Jesus, and the Holy Spirit.

Stay focused! This is revelation, a truth which you may have heard about from preaching, teaching, etc., but not practiced. Before you can practice, you must have the knowledge of the three voices and how to discern which voice is speaking.

---

[26] *https:// www.amazon.com/How-Know-Voice-God-Speak-ebook/dp/B07326618H*

Before we continue, I want to emphasize this again to help you stay focused on the part you are to play. Remember, Christianity is *doing* and *practicing*, not just *hearing only*. (James 1:22)

The junk in our souls must be traded for the things of the spirit if you are going to hear from God by the Holy Spirit. You will hear me reiterate this repeatedly. It has to become a lifestyle of living. We are to *live out* the gospel! Right?

Identifying the Three Voices

#1 - The Human Voice

The first voice we need to recognize and identify is our own human voice or the voice of our human-ness. Some refer to this voice as the flesh or carnal nature of man. Human nature refers to the distinguishing characteristics which include ways of thinking, feeling and acting.

Your voice will sound like your voice, having the same inflections, and will blubber about your own previous fleshly desires. However, the Word of God gives us clear instructions.

> *Do not love the world or the things in the world. If anyone loves the world, the love of the Father is not in him. [16]For all that is in the world—the lust[27] [desires] of the flesh, the lust [desires] of the eyes, and the pride of life [pride in possessions][28] —is not of the Father but is of the*

---

[27] *Strong's Concordance G1939 epigumia, a longing (especially for what is forbidden: concupiscence, desire, lust (after).*
[28] *English Standard Version (ESV) The Holy Bible, English Standard Version. ESV® Text Edition: 2016. Copyright © 2001 by Crossway Bibles, a publishing ministry of Good News Publishers. ESV reference [a] 1 John 2:16 or pride in possessions*

world. ¹⁷And the world is passing away, and the lust [desire] of it; but he who does the will of God abides forever. (Emphasis added)

1 John 2:15-17 (NKJV)

God created humans with five senses! They are taste, touch, smell, hearing and seeing. These five senses all report to the carnal fleshly human mind, which is the enemy of God.

The lust of the flesh (scripture above) includes tasting, touching, smelling and hearing. The lust of the eyes is *seeing*!

The pride of life is *thinking* you are special because of who you are, what you have, what you know or what you look like.

2 Corinthians 10:4-6 states that we have weapons that are not carnal. The term "not carnal" according to *Easton's Bible Dictionary,* simply means *"they are not of man's device, not wielded by human power."* Dictionary.com's definition says 1) *pertaining to or characterized by the flesh or the body, its passions and appetites; sensual* 2) *not spiritual; merely human.*

*We use God's mighty weapons, not worldly weapons, to knock down the strongholds of human reasoning and to destroy false arguments. ⁵We destroy every proud obstacle that keeps people from knowing God. <u>We capture their rebellious thoughts and teach them to obey Christ.</u> ⁶And after you have become fully obedient, we will punish everyone who remains disobedient. (*Emphasis added*)*

2 Corinthians 10:4-6 (NLT2)

Another passage from Romans 8:6-8 tells us that *"to be carnally [not spiritual; merely human] minded is death; but to be spiritually minded [having the mind set on spiritual things; filled with holy desires and purposes: spiritual[29]] is life and peace.* (Emphasis added)

Learning the differences between your human voice, God's voice, and satan's voice can be the difference between having a life of peace and joy even in the midst of trouble or trials.

Traits of the Human Voice

So I say, let the Holy Spirit guide your lives. Then you won't be doing what your sinful nature craves. [17]The sinful nature wants to do evil, which is just the opposite of what the Spirit wants. And the Spirit gives us desires that are the opposite of what the sinful nature desires. These <u>two forces are constantly fighting each other</u>, so <u>you are not free to carry out your good intentions</u>. [18]But when you are directed by the Spirit, you are not under obligation to the law of Moses. [19]<u>When you follow the desires of your sinful nature, the results are very clear: sexual immorality, impurity, lustful pleasures, [20]idolatry, sorcery, hostility, quarreling, jealousy, outbursts of anger, selfish ambition, dissension, division, [21]envy, drunkenness, wild parties</u>, and <u>other sins like these</u>. Let me tell you again, as I have before, that anyone living that sort of life will not inherit the Kingdom of God. (Emphasis added)

Galatians 5:16-21 (NLT2)

For I am afraid that perhaps when I come I may find you to be not what I wish and may be found by you to be not what you wish; that perhaps there will be <u>strife, jealousy, angry tempers, disputes, slanders, gossip, arrogance, disturbances</u>; (Emphasis added)

2 Corinthians 12:20 (NASB)

---

[29] [29] https://www.merriam-webster.com/dictionary/spiritually-minded

But for the <u>cowardly and unbelieving</u> and <u>abominable</u> <u>and murderers</u> and <u>immoral persons</u> and <u>sorcerers</u> and <u>idolaters</u> and <u>all liars</u>, their part will be in the lake that burns with fire and brimstone, which is the second death. (Emphasis added)

Revelation 21:8 (NASB)

Since they thought it foolish to acknowledge God, he abandoned them to their foolish thinking and let them do things that should never be done. ²⁹Their lives became full of every kind of <u>wickedness, sin, greed, hate, envy, murder, quarreling, deception, malicious behavior,</u> and <u>gossip</u>. ³⁰They are <u>backstabbers, haters of God, insolent, proud,</u> and <u>boastful</u>. They invent new ways of sinning, and they <u>disobey their parents</u>. ³¹They <u>refuse to understand, break their promises, are heartless, and have no mercy</u>. ³²They know God's justice requires that those who do these things deserve to die, yet they do them anyway. Worse yet, they encourage others to do them, too. (Emphasis added)

Romans 1:28-32 (NLT)

Here are the traits of the human voice based on Galatians 5:16-21. Remember that actions done with the body begin with a *thought* in the head (soul, mind, will, and emotions) The battle is truly in the mind. So, this list is a thought list as well as actions completed by the body given from the instructions of the mind. This is a partial listing as seen above in the scriptures.

1. Sexual immorality
2. Impurity
3. Lustful pleasures
4. Idolatry

5. Sorcery
6. Hostility
7. Quarreling
8. Jealousy
9. Outbursts of anger
10. Selfish ambition
11. Dissension
12. Division
13. Envy
14. Drunkenness
15. Wild parties

Your inner human voice becomes easier to recognize with this list. *All thoughts of* sexual immorality, impurity, lustful pleasures, idolatry, sorcery, hostility, quarreling, jealousy, outbursts of anger, selfish ambition, dissension, division, envy, drunkenness and wild parties *are* therefore *identified as your carnal fleshly human inner voice and not satan's voice* which is who most people blame for having these kinds of thoughts.

An old phrase people use to justify these types of thinking and behavior is *"the devil made me do it."* No, the devil did not make you do it. You did not take control of your carnal fleshly thoughts and choose to change them according to the instructions received from the Word of God.

> *We destroy every proud obstacle that keeps people from knowing God. We capture their rebellious thoughts and teach them to obey Christ.* (Emphasis added)
>
> 2 Corinthians 10:5 (NLT)

This is such a powerful truth! When I find myself jealous, angry, or tempted with these thoughts, I must replace them with the truth of God's Word. This is why it is important, as a new Christian believer, (or even someone who has walked with God and still struggles with hearing the voice of their own humanness) to memorize Scripture, know the Word of God, and have it in their heart (spirit).

You must have the counter-truth for the lie that is coming in your thought life.

Mindfulness, according to *Merriam-Webster online dictionary,* is *"a state of awareness."* Step one in this activation is becoming aware of the negative or ugly thoughts that come to you and cause you to act out with your behavior and actions. Sometimes, after the fact thinking says, "Oh I shouldn't have done that." Mindfulness, or being *aware* as the thought comes to you, is what will alert you to ask yourself the question: "Where did that come from? Is this my sinful, fleshly thought?"

Dictionary.com gives the meaning of *mindfulness* as *"a technique in which one focuses one's full attention only on the present, experiencing thoughts, feelings and sensations."* Taking control of your thought-life is one of the *"keys to the gate of hades"* that Jesus gave to His body, the *ekklesia* (church). (Matthew 16:17-19)

Practice the activations to begin learning how to recognize and replace these thoughts of your human voice.

Activation and Training Exercise
Before You Begin

(Read through all the instructions before you begin.)

For as he thinks within himself, so he is.

Proverbs 23:7a (NASB)

I tell you the truth, whatever you <u>bind on earth</u> will be <u>bound in heaven</u>, and whatever you <u>loose on earth</u> will be <u>loosed in heaven</u>. (Emphasis added)

Matthew 18:18 (NIV)

Before you begin to train and change the negative or sinful thoughts for God thought's you need to pray the following prayers of binding and loosening!

One definition of binding from *Webster's Revised Unabridged Dictionary* is *"to make fast (a thing) about or upon something, as by tying; to encircle with something; as to bind a belt about one; to bind a compress upon a part."*

Strong's Talking Greek, Hebrew Dictionary, g3089, means to *"put off, break up, destroy."*

This is exactly how we *loose and bind* God's Word to our mind. We are going to make fast, tie and encircle God's Word to our mind and loose, put off, break up and destroy Satan's control and hold on our minds.

Binding and Loosening Prayer

Satan, thru the power of the Holy Spirit, and by the name of Jesus I loose, smash, crush, and destroy any strongholds and negative thinking.

I tear up and tear apart all forms of defensiveness and denial in my soul.

I lose, smash, crush, and destroy the wrong beliefs, wrong ideas, and misconceptions in my soul which are getting in the way of right thinking.

Lord, I bind my carnal, fleshly mind, my will, and my emotions to Your will and purposes for my life.

I do not want my soul to be able to establish any more hiding places for wrong beliefs and bad attitudes.

I do not want my mind looking for ways to rephrase its fear and its anger.

I do not want my emotions reacting like fireworks or rain clouds.

I obligate my will to Yours, my mind to the Mind of Christ, and my emotions to the healing power of the Holy Spirit.

Father, Your Word says that to repent means to think differently, to change my mind, to regret my sins and change my conduct. I ask You to forgive me for all ungodly, sinful, fleshly desires in my mind that have kept me from becoming all You have destined.

Today, I choose to do this by becoming mindfully aware of my stinking thinking and training my mind to become the mind of Christ, by replacing my carnal fleshly thoughts and human desires to the thoughts and desires of Christ.

I seal, fasten, secure, shut, and close this prayer by the power of the Holy Spirit and in the mighty name of Jesus.

Activation and Training Exercise
Controlling My Human Voice (thoughts)

(Read through all the instructions before you begin.)

Since therefore Christ suffered in the flesh, <u>arm yourselves with the same way of thinking</u>, for whoever has suffered in the flesh has ceased from sin, ²so as to live for the rest of the time in the flesh no longer for human passions but for the will of God. ³For the time that is past suffices for doing what the Gentiles want to do, living in sensuality, passions, drunkenness, orgies, drinking parties, and lawless idolatry. ⁴With respect to this they are surprised when you do not join them in the same flood of debauchery, and they malign you; ⁵but they will give account to him who is ready to judge the living and the dead. (Emphasis added)

1 Peter 4:1-5 ESV[30]

1. Choose a minimum of three names from the list below which describe a problem you are having that you can't control or get victory over. Identify the thought processes that you are struggling with that is being carried out by your body. In other words, people are seeing your outbursts of anger, gossip, jealousy, etc. (*Example: having angry thoughts toward a person and then not being able to control that anger. Demonstrating outwardly by telling that person off, screaming at them, saying things you don't really mean, or ignoring that person and never speaking to them.*)

2. Put them in priority order from the worst to the least. Begin working on Priority #1. Do not go to Priority #2

---

[30] https://www.openbible.info/topics/sins_of_the_flesh

until you have begun to see a change in how you handle it.

3. Find a key-truth scripture that replaces the thought processes you are having that cause you to follow through with your flesh (body).

Example:

- Outbursts of Anger = 1st Priority
- Gossip = 2nd Priority
- Jealously = 3rd Priority

When I hear my thoughts begin to speak anger, gossip toward a person or jealousy, then I would use the following key steps to take control of my human voice.

Steps to Take Control of The Human Voice!

Step 1. Become *mindful* (constantly aware) of the thoughts which are negative.

Step 2. Reject and refuse the thought! Sometimes I will simply say aloud, "No!"

Step 3. Replace it with a truth scripture from God's Word.

The easiest way to control your stinking thinking is to simply speak out loud to yourself and say *"Shut up! Be quiet! I reject that evil or negative thought in the name of Jesus."* (Just make sure you are alone!) Then begin to speak the key truth replacement thought.

TIP: You can also use your Activation and Training Exercise #2: Changing My Mindset! Confession Refusals, in chapter 7 to replace these thoughts.

Choose Three and List them in Priority

- Sexual immorality
- Impurity
- Lustful pleasures
- Idolatry
- Sorcery
- Hostility
- Quarreling
- Jealousy
- Outbursts of anger
- Selfish ambition
- Dissension
- Division
- Envy
- Drunkenness
- Wild parties

Make this Commitment

Daily I will use the following scriptures to combat these issues in my thoughts (soul).

Key Truth Replacement Scripture Thought!

Sin of Flesh	Scripture	Replacement Truth
Sexual immorality impurity lustful pleasure, adultery, prostitution, fornication (which is sexual relations between unmarried individuals), homosexuality, and bestiality.	1 Corinthians 6:19-20 (NLT) Don't you realize that your body is the temple of the Holy Spirit, who lives in you and was given to you by God? You do not belong to yourself, [20]for God bought you with a high price. So, you must honor God with your body.	"I exchange this thought of (list the thought) porn, lust, etc. NOW because my body is the temple of the Holy Spirit and He lives IN me and I belong to Him. I will honor God with my thoughts and my body."
Impurity, physical or moral uncleanness; something that is or that makes impure; adulterant, contaminant, contamination, defilement, pollutant[31]	Matthew 5:8 (NASB) Blessed are the pure in heart, for they shall see God.	"I trade this thought of (list the thought) NOW for the truth which says "I am blessed" because my heart is not impure, contaminated, or defiled

---

[31] *https://www.merriam-webster.com/thesaurus/impurity*

Sin of Flesh	Scripture	Replacement Truth
Sorcery: the use of power gained from the assistance or control of evil spirits especially for divining. Bewitchery, bewitchment, conjuring, devilry (or deviltry), diablerie, enchantment, spells, magic, mojo, necromancy, thaumaturgy, voodooism, witchcraft, witchery, wizardry[32]	Revelation 18:23 (NASB) And the light of a lamp will not shine in you any longer; and the voice of the bridegroom and bride will not be heard in you any longer; for your merchants were the great men of the earth, because all the nations were deceived by your sorcery. Deuteronomy 18:10-12 Malachi 3:5 Revelation 21:8	"I reject the thought of (list the thought) using any type of sorcery, or witchcraft now because it leads to darkness and deception of the true nature of the one true God. It leads to death."
Hostility (Enmity) Deep-seated dislike or ill will; true hatred, either overt or concealed[33]	1 Peter 4:8 (NASB) Above all, keep fervent in your love for one another, because love covers a multitude of sins.	

[32] https://www.merriam-webster.com/thesaurus/sorcery

[33] https://www.merriam-webster.com/dictionary/hostility

Sin of Flesh	Scripture	Replacement Truth
Quarreling, outbursts of anger	2 Timothy 2:23-24 (NLT2) Again I say, don't get involved in foolish, ignorant arguments that only start fights. [24]A servant of the Lord must not quarrel but must be kind to everyone, be able to teach, and be patient with difficult people.	
Jealousy, envy, selfish ambition	James 4:2-3 (NIV) You want something but don't get it. You kill and covet, but you cannot have what you want. You quarrel and fight. You do not have, because you do not ask God. [3]When you ask, you do not receive, because you ask with wrong motives, that you may spend what you get on your pleasures. (Emphasis added from ISV.)	

#2 - Voice of Satan

Be of sober spirit, be on the alert. Your adversary, the devil, prowls around like a roaring lion, seeking someone to devour.

1 Peter 5:8 (NASB)

A necessary skill as a believer in our salvation spiritual walk is to be able to discern who is speaking to us in the depths of our soul (flesh, mind, will, and emotions). Years and years of frustration and confusion will follow us without this training at the beginning of our salvation walk. Each decision we face in life can be greatly affected by not being able to discern whether it is our human nature voice or the enemy of our soul, satan. Therefore, we may need to have a salvation *Re-Start*!

Satan speaks to you in your *soul*! (flesh, mind, will, and emotions) He cannot speak to you in your inner being, your *spirit,* where the Godhead lives. Now that you understand what and how your human voice speaks let us define how satan speaks to us in our head.

All humans have a supernatural enemy whose aim is to use pain and pleasure to make us blind, stupid and miserable. He has many names in the Bible. Just a few are: *the adversary (1 Peter 5:8), the ruler of this world (John 12:31), the accuser (Revelation 12:9-10) and the god of this age (2 Corinthians 4:4).*

Thankfully our heavenly Father has not left us to handle him in our own strength. He has given us *"weapons of warfare"* according to 2 Corinthians 10:4-6. Christ also has already won the battle against satan.

The Son of God appeared...to destroy the works of the devil.

1 John 3:8 (NASB)

Christ took on human nature that through death he might destroy him who has the power of death, that is, the devil. (Emphasis added)

Hebrews 2:14

God disarmed the principalities and powers and made a public example of them, triumphing over them in him. In other words, the decisive blow was struck at Calvary. (Emphasis added)

Colossians 2:15

No one can enter a strong man's house and plunder his goods, unless he first binds the strong man.

Mark 3:27 (ESV)

Revelation 20:10 says one day the warfare will be over: "*The devil [will be] thrown into the lake of fire and brimstone and will be tormented day and night forever and ever.*" (Emphasis added) (See Matthew 8:29; 25:41)

The Way He Speaks!

1. Accusations
2. Blinds the mind of unbelievers to keep them from seeing the light of the gospel.
3. Confusion
4. Condemnation
5. Contradicts God's Word
6. Deception
7. Doubt
8. Fear
9. Lack of peace
10. Lies
11. Poses as an "angel of light"; speaks what your human voice wants to hear.
12. Temptation to sin.

The devil has an army of evil spirits who operate on his behalf. When he or his evil spirits begin speaking to you, they will bring *confusion*. James 3:16 says: *"for where envying and strife is, there is confusion and every evil work."*

Get ready for a revelation! *"God is not the author of confusion."* (1 Corinthians 14:33)

While looking at James 3:16, (KJV) again, it reveals, *"For where envying and strife is, there is confusion and every evil work."*

Ask yourself this question: Whose voice conveys envy and strife? (Come on; you can get this one!) Yes, that's right. It is the voice of *you*—your carnal, fleshly voice.

Now ask another question: Whose voice is confusion? Bingo! That's right! It is the voice of the devil, satan, or his evil cohorts.

Now let's get the revelation of what the scripture is saying to us by looking at some other scriptures.

> Then Jesus said to His disciples, "If anyone desires to come after Me, let him deny himself, and take up his cross, and follow Me."
>
> Matthew 16:24 (NKJV)
>
> That you put off, concerning your former conduct, the old man which grows corrupt according to the deceitful lusts, 23and be renewed in the spirit of your mind, 24and that you put on the new man which was created according to God, in true righteousness and holiness.
>
> Ephesians 4:22-24 (NKJV)
>
> I beseech you therefore, brethren, by the mercies of God, that you present your bodies a living

sacrifice, holy, acceptable to God, which is your reasonable service.

Romans 12:1 (NKJV)

It appears from reading these scriptures that we have some participation in taking control of our human nature voice, the soul (fleshly, mind, will, and emotions).

We must immediately recognize when there are thoughts of envy and thoughts of strife in our heads. This is our own sinful nature, our human voice, trying to gain control of us again. If we do not tell it to go in the name of Jesus and learn how to trade and replace the envy with love and the strife with peace then it opens the door to satan. He then brings confusion and every evil work. Once satan's voice is allowed in the soul, we must then engage it—the confusion and every evil work as it speaks to our soul—on a different level of warfare.

Simply stated, *"Not being mindful of our thoughts, not engaging in training, and not learning how to replace thoughts of our flesh will open the door to satan, who brings confusion and every evil work."*

Believe me when I say that it is easier to deal with one voice at a time. Once satan gains a foothold in your mind, the negative and evil thoughts start coming to you like a tsunami. Instead of a few thoughts, you have thousands! The thoughts begin to overwhelm you. Then you begin to act on those thoughts if you don't get control of them.

If you don't recognize the voice of your carnal, fleshly soul, you will not recognize the voice of the enemy, satan and will blame everything on him.

Why Is Blaming the Devil for Everything Dangerous?

It is a deception of satan's to keep you from seeing that you have weaknesses or faults. Since you blame or fault him with everything, it takes the focus away from you. The result is you will not deal with the issues of your flesh and you will get discouraged when you tell satan to flee, (James 4:7) because he keeps coming back into your thought life.

This means you have not closed the door on that thought by doing the following:

1) Acknowledging you have a weakness (envy, jealousy, strife, unforgiveness, etc.)

2) Being mindful and training yourself to replace those thoughts with truth.

Satan often infiltrates your mind with condemnation. He says, "How can you talk about God to other people when you still have issues of your own?" The truth of the matter says to him: *"You are a liar devil. There is now no condemnation to them which are in Christ Jesus."* (Emphasis added) (Romans 8:1)

One of satan's greatest strategies is fear. The truth resists the thought and says, *"God has not given me a spirit of fear, but of power, love and a sound mind."* (Emphasis added) (2 Timothy 1:7) Go *now, fear,* in the name of Jesus!

Satan always attempts to lure you away from God's commandments. He did this to Adam and Eve in the Garden. He seeks to divide and conquer by creating anxiety rather than peace. The trading truth says that *"He will keep us in perfect peace if our mind is stayed on Him."*

When satan speaks, he comes at you with the opposite of truth. He is the father of lies (John 8:44). He is also the tempter. (Matthew 4:3) He is called the *"accuser of the brothers."* (Revelation 12:10)

The old adage, *"The devil made me do it,"* is a lie. The devil doesn't make you do anything. The Bible says, in James 1:14, (NIV) that *"each person is tempted when they are dragged away by their own evil desire and enticed. Then, after desire has conceived, it gives birth to sin; and sin, when it is full-grown gives birth to death."*

Again, we will examine this scripture and ask some questions: Where are we tempted? Answer: in our thought life.... our soul, mind, will and emotions. Your five senses, seeing, hearing, tasting, smelling and touching produces thoughts. Every action and behavior begin with a thought! Someone said, your thoughts become your words, your words become your actions, and your actions become your habits. Wow!

Our highest calling is to be conformed[34] to the image of Christ. You will not resemble Christ if you have not practiced the key *Re-Start Principles*. Your growth will be stunted, and years later you will question why certain things keep happening to you.

How are we *made to resemble or look like Christ*?

1. By becoming mindful and training yourself to take control of the thoughts in your head made by your human voice and satan's voice;
2. Learning the difference between the voices;
3. Replacing the thoughts quickly with the truth of God's Word. (See #3 God's Voice for a comparison chart on satan's voice and God's voice)

---

[34] *Conform defined = made to resemble; assuming the same form; like; resembling. by KJV Dictionary Definition: conform online*

#3 - The Voice of God

> *That He would grant you, according to the riches of His glory, to be strengthened with might through His Spirit in the inner man, [17]that Christ may dwell in your hearts through faith; that you, being rooted and grounded in love, [18]may be able to comprehend with all the saints what is the width and length and depth and height—[19]to know the love of Christ which passes knowledge; that you may be filled with all the fullness of God. [20]Now to Him who is able to do exceedingly abundantly above all that we ask or think, according to the power that works in us...*

Ephesians 3:16-20 (NKJV)

Before we begin to recognize God's voice, we must first know from where He speaks to us. The three-part man includes the spirit. This happens when we are *saved*. Or another way to say this is that we have been reborn of the Spirit. This rebirth happens in our "inner man." (See chapter 7.) God speaks to us from our inner being—our spirit. (Hebrews 4:12) He doesn't speak in our mind (our soul). His thoughts bypass the mind! They come from a deep place within. Some people express this as: "*I know, that I know, that I know.*" It is a *knowing* that has no thought processes with it.

In order to *know* God's Voice, we must be well-trained in hearing and knowing the voice of our human-ness and the voice of satan. Many people have been misled by mistaking the voice of satan, who can masquerade as an angel of light, for the voice of God. (2 Corinthians 11:14) Listening carefully for the voice of God is necessary because His voice is not the only voice that speaks. Being led away by our own imaginings or fooled by the voice of satan is a serious thing.

Many foolish choices have been made by those who think

they have heard the voice of God. My husband and I attended a church once where a man in the congregation told everyone, "God told me to divorce my wife and marry someone else's wife." He divorced his wife and broke up the marriage of the other woman and married her because he heard the voice of God. He then left the church and the couple married and moved away.

Training is necessary for every believer at the beginning of their walk with Christ. It was many years after my conversion experience before training began in these necessary key principles. Until training was implemented, there was constant confusion regarding which voice was speaking to me. Never fear! It is not too late for you!

Knowing God's voice requires having the Word of God implanted inside of you. God will never violate His Word! (Psalm 89:34-35) Hebrews 6:18 tells us that God can't lie. He can't break an unconditional promise. What He says, He will fulfill! Another scripture tells us that His *Word will not return void (useless, without result)*.

Comparison Chart

How God Speaks!	How Self/Satan Speaks!
In my Innermost being, my spirit 2 Corinthians 4:16; Proverbs 20:27; Colossians 3:10	In my soul, my head, my mind, my will, & thru my emotions Hebrews 4:12
With gentle leadings 2 Corinthians 10:1; James 3:17	Clamoring, loud demands of self or satan 1 Kings 19:11-13
Produces freedom John 8:36	Produces bondage Matthew 11:28-30
When we are seeking Him Matthew 7:7-8; Jeremiah 29:12-13	Speaks with sudden intrusions of thoughts into the mind 2 Corinthians 10:4-5; Ephesians 6:11
A definite sense that everything is under control Philippians 4:6-7	Things are out of control 1 Corinthians 10:13
Gives clear-cut, specific directions Proverbs 3:6	Communicates in confusion, uncertain wonderings 1 Corinthians 14:33
Convicts of specific sins John 16:8	Accuses in broad generalities that leave a sense of guilt and condemnation Revelation 12:10
Speaks with 100% truth that can be tested by the Word of God John 14:6	Speaks lies, deceit, and half-truths John 8:44;
Always leads to peace Philippians 4:7	Peace is absent 2 Corinthians 2:11
Never speaks contrary to His Word John 12:49-50; John 16:13-15	Causes to question God Genesis 3:1

The activations included in all chapters will help you in this journey to hear and know when God is speaking to you.

9

WATER BAPTISM RE-START PRINCIPLE

Therefore, if anyone is in Christ, he is a new creation; old things have passed away; behold, all things have become new.

2 Corinthians 5:17 (NKJV)

I have been crucified with Christ; it is no longer I who live, but Christ lives in me; and the life which I now live in the flesh I live by faith in the Son of God, who loved me and gave Himself for me.

Galatians 2:20 (NKJV)

The second place in our *Re-Start* happens in water baptism. There are seven baptisms mentioned in the scriptures but we want to deal with the water baptism of Jesus, commonly known as our Christian baptism. (Matthew 3:13-17)

Water baptism is considered one of the tenets of the Christian faith. For many years I looked at this experience as just that...something you are to do after you become born again. The reason *why* was because that's what Jesus did, so we do what He did. Needless to say, having that kind of mindset might keep one from understanding the truth of what water baptism really means.

Another mindset believes water baptism is a symbolic outward representation of being born again, by relating what happens in baptism to Christ's death, burial, and resurrection. (Romans 6:3-4)

In *acting out* Jesus death, burial, and resurrection we are:

1. Put in a tomb or a grave with Him
    *   The minister places us under the water.
    *   Signifies our death with Jesus.
2. Risen from the grave with him
    *   The minister brings us up out of the water.
    *   Signifies our resurrection with Jesus.

This is a beautiful picture and act of relating to Christ in His death, burial, and resurrection. We don't want to diminish the power of it, but there are more than the two mindsets that have been mentioned.

Many people today have missed the principle in water baptism and therefore are like the Israelite children, wandering around the desert trying to figure out who they are and what purpose they have in life. What in the world does water baptism have to do with finding out who I am and what my purpose is in life?

Everything!

If we don't understand the principle of water baptism, it means that we have not trained ourselves regarding water baptism.

Baptize, in the Greek, means *"to immerse; cover wholly with a fluid, or fully wet."* In the gospel account of Mark 1:9-11 Jesus is baptized by John *"in the Jordan river."*

Small words can be very significant.

Follow along with me: *in* is a preposition. Prepositions are words usually used in front of nouns or pronouns and they show the relationship between the noun or pronoun and other words in a sentence.[35] The word *in* refers to the element in which you are immersed. In this case, it was immersion in the Jordan river.

In Romans 6:3 we read, *"Or do you not know that as many of us as were baptized into Christ Jesus were baptized into His death?"* (speaking of water baptism) In this verse, another small word which is significant is the word *into* meaning the product or result of being immersed.

What did we miss practicing in water baptism? Let's connect the dots. The truth we must accept in water baptism is that we begin to behave, think, and become the end product or final result — the nature and identity, the persona, of Christ, as we go *in* or *into* the element in which we are immersed.

The Identity Thief

> The thief does not come except to steal, and to kill, and to destroy. I have come that they may have life, and that they may have it more abundantly.

> John 10:10 (NKJV)

Identity theft is also known as identity fraud. It is a crime in which an imposter steals your identity by obtaining pieces of your personal information. Once they receive your personal information, they can do almost anything in your name including make charges on your credit cards, open new accounts, drain your bank account and even pay for medical treatment on your health insurance. I've read they can even file a tax refund in your name and get your refund. The identity thief's power is unlimited.

This is exactly what satan has done to believers regarding

---

[35] *https://en.oxforddictionaries.com/prepositions/*

water baptism. He has come and stolen an important truth in water baptism. It has to do with *identity*!

One of the most important revelations we can receive from the Word of God is to understand who we are in Christ. Understanding who we are and knowing how we see ourselves is our identity.

Why is it important for us to know our identity in Christ?

Answer: Identifying with Christ will change the way we live and cause us to rise above adversity. Not understanding our identity or how we see ourselves in Him keeps us living far below our rights and privileges in Christ.

I was water baptized as a young child. Even if my parents had explained to me the significance and importance of baptism, it did not compute. Some of you were probably baptized as children and don't remember it as anything except as something done after receiving Jesus in our heart. Much time was wasted in my life because I did not know who I was in Christ! Remember, my mindset regarding the act of water baptism had nothing to do with identity. It was a ritual, the thing we were to do after salvation. Maybe you can relate to what I am saying right now.

What a mess! As a young adult, I had a weak relationship with God and certainly did not know that humans were created a three-part being—spirit, soul, and body. Lack of spiritual knowledge produced an inability to distinguish between the three voices that speak to humans. Grumbling, griping, whining and crying became a way of life simply because I didn't know who in the world I was. I excused my own weakness and felt as if no one loved me. I believed no one cared about me. I made myself feel better by convincing myself that others were to blame. Insecurity became the blanket that covered my shoulders. My feelings were constantly being hurt because others didn't understand me. There was this ache inside of me that constantly looked to others for acceptance and affirmation. Acceptance and affirmation only can come into your heart when you know who you are in Christ.

Every day we identify with people, our jobs, our church, or an organization. Some identify with their profession. They say things like, "I'm a carpenter," or "I'm a doctor," or "I'm a CEO," or "I'm a pastor." But their profession is not who they are; it is what they do.

Many people identify with the disease or sickness that is attacking their bodies. They say, "I'm a diabetic," or "I'm bipolar." Others have allowed people to define them by telling them who they are and who they aren't. I spoke earlier that my husband was told when he was growing up, "You aren't worth the salt in cornbread." He could have allowed himself to be defined by that statement which was repeated to him many times. Instead, he said, "No, that is not who I am. Just watch and see! I'll show you that I am worth more than the salt in the cornbread." He educated himself, worked hard, and eventually opened two retail tire stores in two cities and a major brand truck tire retread plant. He became the second largest dealer for a major tire distributor in the southeast. He knew who he was!

We tend to judge personal worth by external factors—race, gender, possessions, accomplishments, education, and even job titles. So, we try to be someone we are not. Even our culture struggles with many forms of identity, race and gender to mention just a few. This is not your Identity! This is a mistaken identity!

Identity Crisis

The Body of Christ is having an identity crisis! The *Google dictionary* online says that identity is *the fact of being who or what a person or thing is.*[36] There is so much confusion as to how Christians see themselves or what kind of people they are to be. They are uncertain about their feelings about themselves, their character, and their goals. They listen to one sermon telling them, "This is who you are in Christ," and another minister says, "No, this is what and who you are in Christ."

Who You Really Are

> *Who you are is far more than what you see on the outside!*

Who you are is far more than what you see on the outside. Most people look at the outward appearance. You are created in the image of God (Genesis 1:27) and are uniquely and wonderfully made. (Psalm 139:13-14) Mankind received his identity—how he saw himself—from God in the garden. His identify was to be like God. Mankind lost his identity after he sinned and only a renewed relationship with Jesus Christ can restore the way man properly sees himself. We are called to be new creatures (2 Corinthians 5:17).

Salvation is far more than just a one-time occurrence. It is an active ongoing process in which God renews, sanctifies and transforms us to be more like Him. We must constantly renew our minds according to His truth instead of our fallen sinful nature (Romans 12:2) and recognize our worth in God's eyes and understand the extent of His love for us. We are called to be imitators of God. (Ephesians 5:1-2 NKJV)

---

[36] *http://googledictionary.freecollocation.com/meaning?word=identity*

Our three-part being, comprised of spirit, soul and body gives us insight into who we really are. We have a physical body and a soul (mind, will and emotions) which relate to the world around us through our five senses. Our inner self, our spirit, is connected to God and is in perfect relationship with God. The apostle Paul writes about this in 2 Corinthians 4:16, (NIV) and says, "*Though outwardly we are wasting away, yet inwardly we are being renewed day by day.*" Our goal is to get our actions, attitudes and behaviors to match up with who is on the inside of us.

Water baptism is more than a symbolic act. I love the way Galatians 3:27-28 (NIV) expresses what happens. Verse 27 says, "*for all of you who were baptized into Christ have clothed yourselves with Christ.*"

1 Peter 2:9 (NIV) says: "*You are a chosen people, a royal priesthood, a holy nation, God's special possession, that you may declare the praises of Him who called you out of darkness into His wonderful light.*"

What are these scriptures describing? First, Galatians is saying that you must embrace your new identity every morning just like you put on your clothes for the day. You must *clothe* yourself with the new identity, the new mindset! (See Chapter 7: Activation: Changing My Mindset)

Identity: the way you see yourself, the fact of being who or what a person or thing is, Christ.

Secondly, 1 Peter describes the new nature, the new identity, the way you must begin to see yourself! You are a chosen people, a royal priesthood, a holy nation, God's special possession.

If you continue to think that you are no good, you will probably live as if you are no good. Trading must take place. (Chapter 7: Activation: Changing My Mindset)

Regardless of what your head says to you, regardless of how you are defined by others, you are not defined by your mistakes, your experiences, your behaviors or your talents. This is not your Identity! Halleluiah! You are a brand-new creature in Christ!

Change Your Identity

Have you ever wanted to erase your life and start over? There are movies and books about people who change their identity and start life over as someone else. People have done this by creating a new name and a new address by moving to a new location far away from their origin.

Recently, a friend told me about a person who pretended to be something he was not. He befriended a female senior citizen and pretended to love her. He then married the lady, started charging on her credit cards, sold her car, and emptied her bank account. He was beginning to do the same things to another elderly lady in another state by using a different name and a different identity. Sad but true story! He was a fraud. Even sadder is the fact that the elderly lady was presented with proof of his fraud and still decided to stay with this man. She made a choice.

You also have a choice today to *Re-Start* and begin life anew, growing in grace and admonition of the Lord.

The Wrong Identity Will Lead to Failure!

Here is what happens when you are born again of the Spirit. Your new self in Christ is here forever. You possess eternal life right now because you are in Christ! Being a Christian is not simply getting a ticket to heaven. No, you receive a brand-new nature (2 Corinthians 5:17). Old things have passed away and all things have become new. You exchanged your old nature and identity for your new divine identity, nature. Water baptism brings this new identity in Christ. Receiving Jesus as your Lord changes you into someone who did not exist before.

It is not what you do as a Christian that determines who you are; it is who you are that determines what you do. (Ephesians 2:10; 1 Peter 2:9-10)

Understanding your identity, the way you see yourself, will determine how successful you are at living the Christian life. Before you came to Christ, you had the old identity. It is described in Ephesians 2:1-3.

> *And you He made alive, who were dead in trespasses and sins, ²in which you once walked according to the course of this world, according to the prince of the power of the air, the spirit who now works in the sons of disobedience, ³among whom also we all once conducted ourselves in the lusts of our flesh, fulfilling the desires of the flesh and of the mind, and were by nature children of wrath, just as the others.*
>
> Ephesians 2:1-3 (NKJV)

A New Identity

At water baptism, we receive a new identity! This is the new you, the new life. No longer must you figure out and wonder who you are! The new identity means you have taken on the persona (person) of Jesus Christ. Your identity is His identity! What is true about Jesus now applies to you because you are in Christ! It is part of your new identity. Start talking like Him! Start acting like Him …. because you are in water baptism.

> *Therefore we were buried with Him through baptism into death, that just as Christ was raised from the dead by the glory of the Father, even so we also should walk in newness of life.*
>
> Romans 6:4 (NKJV)

Some would say, "I knew that." Well, if you knew it, then why did you question who you were and where you were going your whole life?

There is a difference in head knowledge and heart knowledge. Head or mind knowledge is having information! Education is wonderful but only of value when you put it into practice. Information is powerful but information or knowledge alone does not transform lives.

Heart or spirit knowledge is the revelation knowledge that comes from your inner man and the new identity of Christ in you, the hope of glory. (1 Corinthians 14:26; Eph 1:17) It is knowledge applied with understanding and revelation. (Proverbs 2:2, 6; 3:13)

His or Mine?

Whose identity do you choose? Will it be the identity of your old self before Christ controlled by voices of your human nature or the accusations of the devil? Here are a few examples of your old identity. You *think* these things about yourself.

Mistaken Identity

(not a complete listing)

- Not smart
- Depressed
- Afraid
- Fearful
- Prideful
- Unloved
- Ugly
- Rejected
- Betrayed

- Controlling
- Unforgiving
- Un-Disciplined
- Sick
- Judgmental
- In-Secure
- Loneliness
- Depressed
- Jealous

If you relate to any of these statements, you have identity issues! Rejecting these types of identities releases you into the identity of Christ and into the *Re-start Principle* of beginning fresh and new. You must begin to see yourself as God sees you. It takes being mindful of negative thoughts and feelings and trading the old nature for His new nature to see yourself through His eyes.

Now let's see what we appear as when clothing ourselves with His identity. When you read these *I am* statements aloud, there will be an immediate lift in your heart.

Identity in Christ Affirmations

I am like Christ	1 John 4:10
I am a child of God	John 1:12
I am loved	1 John 3:3
I am redeemed and forgiven	Colossians 1:14
I am seated in Heavenly places with Christ	Ephesians 2:6
I am chosen of God, holy and dearly loved	Colossians 3:12
I am more than an overcomer	Romans 8:37
I am free from guilt and condemnation	Romans 8:1
I am an overcomer in this life	John 16:33
I am free of fear	2 Timothy 1:7
I am blameless and free from accusation	Colossians 1:22
I am made complete in Christ	Colossians 2:10
I am a son/daughter of light and not darkness	1 Thessalonians 5:5
I am healed	1 Peter 2:24
I am victorious through Jesus Christ	1 Corinthians 15:57
I am an enemy of the devil	1 Peter 2:11
I am forgiven	1 John 2:12
I am fearfully and wonderfully made	Psalm 139:14

Trading our old identity for His identity is the way to success! It opens an entirely new level of Christian living. This results in a death to our old life and marks our new identity in Christ.

The Result of Your New Identity

There are four passages in the Gospels that describe the results of receiving a new identity in Christ. Receiving this new understanding, training your soul (mind, will, and emotions) and walking in your new identity is key in accessing heaven.

Results in the Four Gospels Chart

(Comparison text)

Matthew 3:16-17	Mark 1:10-11	Luke 3:21-22	John 1:28-34
1. Heavens opened to Him Genesis 28:13 Ezekiel 1:26-28 Matt. 3:16-17 Acts 7:54-55	Heavens split open	Jesus was praying and Heaven was opened	From heaven
2. He saw the Spirit of God descending like a dove & coming upon Him	He (John) saw the Spirit descending like a dove into (or unto) Him	Holy Ghost descended in a bodily shape like a dove upon Him	I (John) saw the Spirit descending like a dove and it abode upon Him
3. Voice from the heavens	Voice came from the heavens	Voice came from heaven	
4. This is my beloved Son in whom I am well pleased	Thou art my beloved Son; in thee I am well pleased	Thou art my beloved Son; in thee I am well pleased	God had said to John: Upon whom you shall see the Spirit descending, and remaining on Him, the same is He which baptizeth with the Holy Ghost I saw and bear record: This is the Son of God

Result #1 Heaven (A Portal) Will Be Opened to You

Jesus was praying and heaven was opened! An open heaven means that we have been given access to God who supplies all our needs according to His riches in Christ Jesus. He leads us into His will for our lives. An open heaven means He hears our prayers, our words to Him, and He is listening! Heaven opening or a portal opening signifies new revelation being imparted. Heaven opening signifies we are receiving direction and insights (revelation) which moves us into *deeper levels of Him*.

The Godhead—Father, Son and Holy Spirit—were all present at the water baptism of Jesus. What is the significance of the Godhead showing up at the baptism of Jesus? The revelation is that 100% of the Godhead's presence is with *us,* and they will never leave us from the point of water baptism! *He will never leave you nor forsake you.* (Hebrews 13:5) Awesome!

Result #2 The Dove of Peace Anchors You

The dove—a symbol of the Holy Spirit, our comforter and teacher—brings the spirit of peace that anchors us in the storms of life. Roman vessels carried several anchors which were attached to the stern as well as to the prow.[37] *Wikipedia* states, *"an anchor is a device, normally made of metal, used to connect a vessel to the bed of a body of water to prevent the craft from drifting due to wind or current."*

Significant to the anchor is a phrase "putting down an anchor," which represents the safe end of a long journey. Applying it spiritually the word is used "for that which supports or keeps one steadfast in the time of trial or of doubt." It is an emblem of hope, according to Hebrews 6:19.

---

[37] *Dictionaries - Easton's Bible Dictionary - Anchor*

Understanding the truth of identity in water baptism establishes an anchor in our lives. Hebrews 6:19 (NIV) says, *"We have this hope as an anchor for the soul, firm and secure."* Accepting the new identity in water baptism anchors us at the beginning of our Christian walk and represents the safe end of a long journey—our lifetime of living in His identity.

Due to the current conditions of our lives, His identity prevents us from drifting and supports or keeps us steadfast in our doubts and weaknesses (Ephesians 4:14).

Result #3 You Know the Voice of God

In the salvation *Re-Start Principle,* you have been training to recognize the three voices that are speaking to you. Recognizing which voice is speaking is to know and remember something because of previous knowledge or experience (your training). Hearing and knowing are two different actions. Hearing defined by *Merriam-Webster Dictionary* is *"the act or power of taking in sound through the ear: the sense by which a person hears.* Knowing is *"to perceive with certainty; to understand clearly; to have a clear and certain perception of truth, fact, or anything that exists. To know a thing pre-includes all doubt or uncertainty of its existence."* [38]

Someone said, "God is speaking all the time." Training to hear God's voice is necessary for walking our walk as growing up spiritually is commanded by the scriptures (Hebrews 5:12-14; 6:1; 1 Peter 2:2-3; Colossians 2:6-7). Training moves us from hearing to knowing! Big Difference!

Result #4 Divine Favor is Flowing in Your Life

What is Favor? Favor has been defined by *Merriam-*

---

[38] *https://av1611.com/kjbp/kjv-dictionary/know.html*

Webster Dictionary as *"approving, consideration or attention."*

Baker's Evangelical Dictionary of Biblical Theology defines favor as *"finding favor means gaining approval, acceptance, or special benefits or blessings".*

Have there been times in your life that it seemed as if everything was going wrong? Nothing you did was working? This could have come from a lack of favor in your life, or spiritually speaking, being out of God's approving consideration or attention. To return to His favor, we simply repent of attempting to do life without Him and without His favor. We should seek for His wisdom (Proverbs 8:35) instead of using our human wisdom.

When we are in the favor of the Lord, many good things will begin to happen.

1) Our prayers and petitions are more likely to be granted. (See above #1 Heaven Will Be Opened to You)
2) Our enemies will not triumph over us (Luke 1:71, 74; 21:15)

Having the favor of God opens the doors to opportunities that we would normally miss by living outside of His favor.

Result #5 You become FULL of His Holy Spirit

(discussed in the next chapter)

After Our New Identity

Now, understanding that we have taken on a new identity, what else do we need to understand about our water baptism?

Ephesians 2:6 (NLT2) gives us insight into the answer. *"For he raised us from the dead along with Christ and underline{seated us with him in the heavenly realms} because we are united with Christ Jesus."* (Emphasis added)

There is that little word *in* again. In case you have forgotten, *in* relates to the element in which you are immersed, and in this case would be *heavenly places*.

God raised us up together and made us sit together in the heavenly places in Christ Jesus. Romans 8:17 tells us we are *"joint heirs or co-heirs with Christ."* The word *sit*, in *Strong's* #4776, means *"to made to sit together."* Sitting denotes a position! Position according to the *dictionary.com* is defined as *"a place occupied or to be occupied; site."*

In and through Christ, we have been re-positioned from an earth's perspective to a heavenly perspective. In other words, our identity is now as the persona (person) of Christ and we operate in the earth realm from the *position of heaven* with Christ Jesus! Now that was a mouthful of revelation! Ding! Ding! The bells are going off.

The Lord's Prayer in Matthew 6:10 (NASB) witnesses to this fact. *"Your kingdom come. Your will be done, on earth as it is in heaven."*

What does this means to us? No more defeated life! No more feeling less than. No more depression! Why? Because we have a new identity that makes us more than conquerors and because we are now living from a position of *"in heaven"* on earth.

We can bring what is in heaven to the earth. There is no lack in heaven! No sickness, sin or disease in heaven! Think about it!

You are not alone in your walk in Christ. Not only are you made in His image and have His identity, but you operate from an invisible realm called heaven. 2 Corinthians 4:18 validates this: *"So we fix our eyes not on what is seen, (in earth) but on what is unseen (heaven), since what is seen (in earth, our problems, faulty self-image, sickness,) is temporary, but what is unseen (in heaven, victory over circumstances, situations, more than conquerors, healing) is eternal."* (Emphasis added)

Why is My Position So Important?

This position of being seated with Him in the heavenly realms is referring to authority and rulership! (Ephesians 1:19-22 (NASB) Position precedes (goes before) power! (More on this in the next chapter.) Let me say

> *Position Always Proceeds Power!*

it again even more definitively. Position *always* precedes power! Without this understanding and training at water baptism, we are *"infants tossed back and forth by the waves, and blown here and there by every wind of teaching and by the cunning and craftiness of people in their deceitful scheming."* (Ephesians 4:14 NIV)

Water baptism identifies me as in Christ, (who I am) and then positions me in the heavenly realm. This gives me the *authority and power* to operate as a child of God. Without position, we live defeated lives. With position, *we can do all things* thru Christ!

ACTIVATION
Identity Repentance Prayer

(Read through all the instructions before you begin.)

1) Find a quiet place to seek the Lord. (You may use quiet instrumental music)
2) Repeat the following identity repentance prayer.

Heavenly Father! I come before You humbly asking for forgiveness for listening to the negative voices and words that have been spoken over my life or by others that have caused me to choose the wrong identity. I make the choice today to forgive myself and others who have participated in making this wrong choice. I release anger and resentment and choose to let all offenses spoken to me by family, friends and others go and will leave it in the hands of God.

Today I receive God's cleansing, love and restoring grace. I renounce all results of choosing self-identity over the identity of Christ. Today, I chose the identity of Christ which says I have value because Jesus gave His life for me. I clothe myself with the identity of Christ and nothing can separate me from God's love (Romans 8:35). My affirmation and identity are chosen and adopted as God's child (Ephesians 1:4-5), and I am sealed with the Holy Spirit. (Ephesians 1:13-14)

ACTIVATION
Renunciations of Self Identity

(Read through all the instructions before you begin.)

Training to *think* differently about yourself is of great importance. Some have years of thinking and hearing from others that they are unloved, rejected, abandoned, etc. The wrong identity will continually attempt to keep us in the same pattern. Renunciations are a great way to reject those thoughts and replace them with God thoughts.

How to Deal with Self-Identity Thoughts/Words

Step 1	Become more mindful (See chapter 7)
Step 2	Reject and renounce the thought as soon as it appears (Use renunciation samples below.)
Step 3	Replace it with what God says about you in the Word of God (See "Identity in Christ Affirmations, Chapter 10: Water Baptism *Re-Start Principle*: His or Mine?)

- RENUNCIATION #1

I renounce the lie that I am rejected, ugly, unloved, dirty or shameful because, *in Christ*, I am completely accepted in the name of Jesus.

- RENUNCIATION #2

I renounce and reject the lie that I am worthless, inadequate, helpless or hopeless because, *in Christ*, I am full of potentiality in the name of Jesus.

- RENUNCIATION #3

I reject and renounce the lie of _____ (*fill in the lie*) in the name of Jesus, because *in Christ*_____ (*fill in your promise*).

ACTIVATION
AFFIRMING MY POSITION

(Read through all the instructions before you begin.)

Use the following positive confessions and repeat until you are secure in your position in Christ.

Position Confessions

- I AM: Blessed with every spiritual blessing in the heavenlies in Christ. (Ephesians 1:3)
- I AM: Seated in heavenly places with Christ, having set my heart on things above where Christ is seated at the right hand of God. (Colossians. 3:1)
- I WILL: Pray from a position of rulership, power and authority. Everything that is His is mine. (Romans 8:17)

I indeed baptize you with water unto repentance, but He who is coming after me is mightier than I, whose sandals I am not worthy to carry. He will baptize you [he will immerse you; He will totally saturate you] with the Holy Spirit and fire. (Emphasis added)

Matthew 3:11 (NKJV)

Now John was clothed with camel's hair and with a leather belt around his waist, and he ate locusts and wild honey. ⁷And he preached, saying, "There comes One after me who is mightier than I, whose sandal strap I am not worthy to stoop down and loose. ⁸I indeed baptized you with water, but He will baptize you with the Holy Spirit."

Mark 1:6-8 (NKJV)

Behold, I send the Promise of My Father upon you; but tarry in the city of Jerusalem until you are endued with power from on high.

Luke 24:49 (NKJV)

And they were all filled with the Holy Spirit and began to speak with other tongues, as the Spirit gave them utterance.

Acts 2:4 (NKJV)

And do not be drunk with wine, in which is dissipation; but be filled with the Spirit.

Ephesians 5:18 (NKJV)

10

<u>HOLY SPIRIT BAPTISM</u>
<u>RE-START PRINCIPLE</u>

It was hot that morning—over 98 degrees. No wind blowing; just dead heat. The air was heavy and the air conditioner was working overtime to keep up with the temperature. Looking out the kitchen bay windows, I noticed the skies began to darken. Hurriedly, I went to the back porch to watch the skies, hoping for a fresh breeze or rain. I found myself settling down on one of the swings as the sky darkened and was lit up by lightning bolts. Jagged bolts of lightning began flashing across the sky. At first, it appeared to be a heat storm. Heat lightning is described as flashes that are too far away from you to hear the thunder. These types of storms with lightning are common in the South.

You could see the electrical static spark in each bolt. What an amazing and breathtaking sight to behold. Zapp! All around me the lightning lit up the skies. The powerful burst of electricity was creating a light show. Before I knew it, thunder began rolling across the skies—the sound of lightning splitting air.

Something in the atmosphere changed. Gusts of wind began to blow across the back porch, seemingly out of nowhere. It was swirling, angry and noisy. As I watched this phenomenon, my mind said, *"Girl, you better go inside. This is not playing around. That lighting is serious and now look what's happening—thunder, and wind."*

I wanted to run into the safety of my family room but felt a check on the inside of me. A small voice said, "Stay." The voice was known to me. After all, I had practiced hearing and knowing whose voice was speaking. It was the still small voice of God coming from deep within my spirit. Running was not an option. My heavenly Father had spoken!

Lightning! Thunder! Wind! Can you guess what came next? Of course, you can. It was the rain. Not just straight down rain, but busy, blowing with the wind, coming from every direction kind of rain. My position on the swing no longer offered me protection from the wind and the rain. It began to blow across the back porch and soak me. It was then I sensed an approval to move into the safety of my home.

After coming inside, I began to hear the Spirit of God speak to me regarding the storm. I will attempt to describe it for you.

The lightning with the electrical sparks in it represented empowerment with fire. It has been defined as *"a life-threatening or shocking turn of events beyond one's control, sudden change or spiritual transformation."*[39] Thunder—a loud rumbling or crashing noise—can shake or vibrate the ground and represents a power discharge in the Spirit. Wind is a sign of the coming Holy Spirit (Acts 2:4). The rain speaks of an outpouring of Holy Spirit Baptism of Fire. (Acts 1:8)

God spoke to me and said, *"My people do not understand the baptism of my Holy Spirit and fire. Many have wandered in darkness not comprehending. There has been great debates and discussions on the Holy Spirit and fire which have caused division among my people. The storm is a picture of what I am about to do in the earth realm. My fire is going to come swiftly and transform the lives of my servants who are searching and*

---

[39] "A-Z Dream Symbology Dictionary, Dr. Barbie L. Breathitt, p 248, Lightning"

seeking for me with their whole hearts. It will begin as flashes, but will then gain power as the thunder, through vibration, will shake the very foundations that believers, ministries, and denominations have built upon. The wind of my Holy Spirit, my breath, the ruach hakodesh, will spontaneously, uncontrollably blow with the rain falling without measure in crazy chaotic drops upon my sons and my daughters.

Theology attempted to place the baptism of the Holy Spirit and fire into a system of religious belief and human interpretation; a box which caused much debate among my people to the point of division. There is no division in the Word! Everything fits together as the three-stranded cord. Unveiling and revelation are on the way to earth even now in those chosen to carry this message regarding the baptism of My Holy Spirit and fire. Take off the restraints of your theological belief system. Open your spiritual eyes and ears to hear what my heart is speaking in these days in which you are now living. Fire! Fire! Fire...has been kindled in the earth and is now ready to burst into flames of Holy Spirit conviction to turn the hearts of my people back to Me, says the Lord. Lightning, thunder, wind, and rain are released now upon the earth!"

The Three Baptism's

The baptisms we are most familiar with are 1) the baptism of John, Jesus' baptism, known as the Christian baptism, 2) water baptism, and 3) the Holy Spirit and fire Baptism.

John the Baptist proclaimed in Mark 1 and John 1, that Jesus *"will baptize in the Holy Spirit."* In Matthew 3 and Luke chapter 3 he proclaimed that Jesus *"will baptize with Holy Spirit and fire."* Both statements, *"will baptize with the Holy Spirit,"* and *"will baptize with the Holy Spirit and fire,"* are keys to our understanding this third *Re-Start* Holy Spirit Principle.

The Story of a King

Image for a moment a king from the Middle Ages. Try to imagine his environment: the castle, the knights and ladies in waiting, the battles, the kingdom and his glory. The king's word was law and his judgments were final. A good king understood that his responsibility was to protect those who lived within his kingdom boundaries; he was also in charge of pursuing the interests of the kingdom by extending its borders and securing additional resources.

The king was granted extraordinary power—at times even absolute power!

Now imagine this sort of king rejecting or being completely unaware of the power that comes with his position as king. What would happen to his kingdom? Soon it would be conquered, its inhabitants enslaved, and its resources confiscated.

It isn't enough for the king to simply hold the position of royalty, meaning he enjoys residence in the palace and the rich lifestyle. He must perform the functions of kingship that are only made possible by the power of his position. The king's position of authority is of no effect if he does not use the power that comes with it.

You say, "What does this have to do with me here and now?"

My response is: *"Everything!"*

As children of God, according to Romans 8:17, we have become co-heirs with Christ. An heir is a person who inherits or has the right to inherit property after the death of its owner. Jesus died and left us this inheritance of the kingdom. In fact, together with Christ, we are heirs of God's glory.

This position is again made clear in Ephesians 2:6: "*For he raised us from the dead along with Christ and seated us with him in the heavenly realms because we are united with Christ.*"

God has raised us up together and made us sit together in the heavenly places in Christ Jesus. In and through Christ, we have been re-positioned. As heirs in this kingdom, we have been charged with the advancement of our Lord's mission.

Let's go back to the image of the king! If we are to be effective in our position in Christ, we must discover and use the power that comes with it.

This story of the king is the story of every born-again believer. We have inherited a kingdom and are kings in this present life. Our mandate is to rule and take dominion, which is the original design in the garden of Eden. (Genesis 1:28)

As kings we are to reign in life, we are to reign over sin, the flesh, circumstances and situations, and over all the power of the enemy (Romans 6:14; Galatians 5:16; Luke 10:19). You are a *kingdom king* and your mandate is to extend the borders of your kingdom and offer protection to its citizens. (Revelation 1:6) You cannot accomplish it without the power of the Holy Spirit and fire!

Position Precedes (goes before) Power!

The last chapter concluded with the statement, "Position precedes (goes before) power." Position and identity are *not* the same! Identity, in water baptism, is the fact of being who or what a person or thing is. Position is the place where someone or something is in relation to other people or things. It is the place where someone or something should be. We must be positioned in Christ before we can ever do anything for His Kingdom. Receiving our identity in Christ at water baptism then places us in the proper position to receive the empowerment of the Holy Spirit.

Imagine Jesus knowing that He is going to the cross and that He will die, be buried, and then resurrected. He will leave planet earth in the hands of His disciples. Three years of His life had been spent walking and talking and instructing the disciples in how to operate as a king in this new kingdom. They didn't fully understand many things but things would begin to make more sense after the death of Jesus. Instructions were necessary for the disciples to carry on. What would happen after He was gone? Who would He leave in charge? Who would guide them?

Words Spoken Before the Resurrection

Jesus gives them a clue in John 14:16-17 and 25-26, as to who He would leave in His absence. (Also check out John 15:26-27; 16:12-16)

> *And I will pray the Father, and He will give you another Helper, that He may abide with you forever—[17]the Spirit of truth, whom the world cannot receive, because it neither sees Him nor knows Him; but you know Him, for He dwells with you and will be in you.*

> *[25]"These things I have spoken to you while being present with you. [26]But the Helper, the Holy Spirit, whom the Father will send in My name, He will teach you all things, and bring to your remembrance all things that I said to you.*

> John 14:16-17, 25-26 (NKJV)

> *And I will ask the Father and he will give you another Savior, the Holy Spirit of Truth, who will be to you a friend just like me—and he will never leave you. The world won't receive him because they can't see him or know him. But you will know him intimately, because he will make his home in you and will live inside you.*

> *I am telling you this while I am still with you. But*
> *when the Father sends the Spirit of Holiness, the*
> *One like me who sets you free, he will teach you*
> *all things in my name. And he will inspire you to*
> *remember every word that I've told you.*

> John 14:16-17, 25-26 (TPT)

These words are very important because they reveal so much to us. He is telling them ahead of time, while He is still with them, that a helper will come after He is gone from the earth. The word *helper* is the Greek word *parakletos*. This word has a legal dimension and refers to one who would be an advocate. In a broader sense, it speaks of comfort, of protection, of counsel and guidance.

He, the Holy Spirit. is a person and was not in the earth *until* Jesus ascended to heaven. This statement is key to our understanding of the baptism of Holy Spirit and fire.

Jesus again tells His disciples that it is to their advantage that He goes away, for if He does not go away, the Helper, the person of the Holy Spirit, will not come to them. But when He goes, He will send the Holy Spirit to them. (John 16:7)

Words Spoken After the Resurrection!

Here is what He spoke to them after the resurrection and before He ascended to heaven.

> *Behold, I send the Promise [pledge][40] of My*
> *Father upon you; but tarry in the city of Jerusalem*

---

[40] *My emphasis Strong's Talking Dictionary G1861 Root*

until you are endued [clothed]⁴¹ with power [mighty, miracle, strength]⁴² from on high."

Luke 24:49 (NKJV)

And being assembled together with them, He commanded them not to depart from Jerusalem, but to wait for the Promise of the Father, "which," He said, "you have heard from Me; ⁵for John truly baptized with water, but you shall <u>be baptized with the Holy Spirit</u> not many days from now." (Emphasis added)

Acts 1:4-5 (NKJV)

He did not suggest that they wait for the promise. He did not recommend that they heed His instruction. He commanded them not to depart from Jerusalem until the promise had come which was the entrance of the Holy Spirit.

> *Empowerment of the Spirit is essential to all kingdom work!*

Jesus was compelled to place such importance on this instruction because empowerment of the Spirit is essential to all kingdom work. In the New Testament gospels, Jesus was baptized in the Spirit and received His anointing and activation to begin His public ministry. He knew His disciples were eager to share the good news of His resurrection and might grow restless waiting for the promise of the Holy Spirit.

Acts 1:3 says, *"To whom He also presented Himself alive after His suffering by many infallible proofs, being seen by them during forty days and speaking of the things pertaining to the*

---

⁴¹ *My emphasis Strong's Talking Dictionary G1746*
⁴² *My emphasis Strong's Talking Dictionary G1410, 1411*

Kingdom of God." In this passage the disciples had spent days with Jesus, hearing Him teach on the Kingdom of God. The Bible states that the apostles had received *"infallible proof"* of His resurrection. They did not need to be persuaded of the validity of their calls because they had first-hand evidence of Christ's victory over death.

In other words, they were ready to get going. But Jesus looked at them and said, (I paraphrase) *"Don't start your ministry! Don't start preaching and teaching the gospel all over the place. Don't start any churches until you have been clothed with the Spirit's power."* (Luke 24:49)

Jesus appeared to the disciples where they were assembled in John 20:19-23. He breathed on them and said, *"Receive you the Holy Ghost."* According to *The Passion Translation,*[43] the word *breathed* does not appear elsewhere in the New Testament. However, it is the same word found in the Septuagint for God *breathed* into Adam's nostrils the breath of life (Genesis 2:7. The beginning of new creation life came from the breath of Jesus, *Re-lifed.* In simple terms, they got *saved*, which is the word known to many in the church. In verse 23, He sends them to preach the forgiveness of sins—and people's sins will be forgiven, but if they don't preach the forgiveness of sins, they will remain guilty. Amazing!

Jesus was preparing the disciples for this *new* Kingdom of God that they were to expand by preaching a gospel of forgiveness.

"Receive you the Holy Spirit." The Greek word for receive means, *"immediately or right now."* They received the infilling of the Spirit inwardly for life, a new life in Christ Jesus—*Re-lifed.*

---

[43] *The Passion Translation, John 20:22, footnote h*

They also needed the outward equipping of power for service on the day of Pentecost.

The Revelation

This is a type or picture of what happens to believers when they receive Jesus Christ as Lord in their life. They receive His new life, His Spirit. He comes into them with a new life, but now they need power for service and to minister.

When we accept Christ as Lord of our Life, we receive the total package of the Godhead-Father, Son and Holy Spirit. But we must begin to activate all that is now living within us by faith. Faith is an action word, meaning that we must physically interact and pursue all of the things living in our new spirit man.

There Is More!

> For this reason I kneel before the Father, [15]from whom his whole family in heaven and on earth derives its name. [16]I pray that out of his glorious riches he may strengthen you with power through his Spirit in your inner being, [17]so that Christ may dwell in your hearts through faith. And I pray that you, being rooted and established in love, [18]may have power, together with all the saints, to grasp how wide and long and high and deep is the love of Christ, [19]and to know this love that surpasses knowledge—that you may be filled to the measure of all the fullness of God.

> Ephesians 3:14-19 (NIV)

In the Old Testament, fire often symbolized the presence of God. What the author of Acts described as wind and tongues as of fire are the manifestations or signs of God's presence. These men and women were engulfed or baptized in God's presence.

132

When the Day of Pentecost had fully come, they were all with one accord in one place. ²And suddenly there came a sound from heaven, as of a rushing mighty wind, and it filled the whole house where they were sitting. ³Then there appeared to them divided tongues, as of fire, and one sat upon each of them. ⁴And they were all filled with the Holy Spirit and began to speak with other tongues, as the Spirit gave them utterance.

Acts 2:1-4 (NKJV)

One writer described the word *"filled"* in Acts 2:4 as meaning *satiated*. The word satiates, according to the *Free on-Line English Dictionary,* means to supply with something to excess. Those in the upper room were filled to excess with the Holy Spirit! All of them experienced a greater degree of God's manifest presence in their lives which produced power to minister.

Albert Barnes' Notes on the Whole Bible describes *"filled"* as "all faculties are pervaded by it, engaged in it, or under its influence." (Acts 3:10; 5:17; 13:45; 2:4)

Manifestation

Another manifestation of *"being filled to excess,"* was the fact that the believer began to speak in other tongues,[44] in addition to the manifestation of wind and fire. Simply stated, a manifestation is when something spiritual becomes real and visible. A sign, according to *The Free Dictionary,* is something that suggests the presence or existence of a fact, condition, or quality. The wind, fire, and speaking in tongues validated Holy

---

[44] *Strong's Talking Dictionary, tongues: G1100 the tongue by implication a language (specially one naturally unacquired)*

Spirit's presence! This was the initial evidence that Holy Spirit power had arrived! There is no refuting this initial baptism of Holy Spirit and fire in Acts 2:1-4, as stated in the Word of God.

Mainline denominations have taught that the only way to receive the baptism of the Holy Spirit and fire is to receive the gift of tongues. I was taught this myself and did experience this phenomenon of speaking in tongues, but I was not seeking the manifestation. I was seeking the Lord, wanting to get closer to Him, wanting *more* of Him, wanting to fill to the excess of Him!

The gift of tongues is one of the nine gifts of the Holy Spirit. (1 Corinthians 12:1-11) Inside our spirit, we have all nine gifts, but each believer is given different *gifts* by the Holy Spirit. Each one of these gifts of the Spirit is a major power gift, and all the gifts are direct, supernatural, miraculous manifestations coming directly from the Holy Spirit Himself. They operate in our lives *as* He *wills* and we *yield*.

In Acts 2:1-4, tongues was given as a manifestation of the Holy Spirit *infilling*. Our focus is not to look at the manifestation which was *speaking in tongues*. If we put our focus on the manifestation that occurred, we will miss what Father God wants to accomplish in us at Holy Spirit Baptism and Fire. For the purpose of this chapter, we are not in any way diminishing speaking in tongues or any visible signs in these occurrences. We want you to place your focus on receiving the Holy Spirit empowerment.

The Revelation

Get it down into your spirit: He has a place for you to become *filled to excess*. Where you receive an overflow of His Spirit with power for ministry which is in you in your newly created spirit man.

So, what is the proof that you are filled to excess? The real proof of this fullness of Christ is stated in the Bible. Read the book of Acts. Miracles, signs and wonders began to be manifested thru the disciples and others who pursued the Lord. It does not say they prayed in tongues before and even after these things happened, but I believe that being fully *satiated* and being supplied with more of the Holy Spirit to excess causes outward, visible things to happen in a person's life.

> *The evidence of the Spirit's presence is given to each person for the common good of everyone.*

> 1 Corinthians 12:7 (GW)

His presence produces evidence!

> *And God confirmed the message by giving signs and wonders and various miracles and gifts of the Holy Spirit whenever he chose.*

> Hebrews 2:4 (NLT2)

This promise of Jesus in Acts 1:5, 8 was fulfilled on the day of Pentecost. He commanded them to wait for the outpouring and they did just that.

Our New Testament command today is simple: *"Be filled with the Spirit."* (Ephesians 5:18) We are clearly recipients of the Holy Spirit but when the tank gets low and you need to fill up your car with gas, you must go to the source and the places that distribute the gas.

To *"be filled with the Spirit"* means that we must spend time in relationship with the Father, the Son Jesus, and the precious Holy Spirit. There are many *"fillings of the Spirit"* that are needful which produce His presence, which produces His power with signs following.

Filling describes an experience that can be repeated. Many times, the disciples were *"filled with the Holy Spirit"* and there was no mention of tongues, (other languages) being spoken. Look it up! (Acts 4:8, 31; 6:3; 7:55; 9:17, 11:24, 13:9, 13:52)

In the baptism of Jesus, we see the heavens open and the Spirit descending like a dove and alighting on Him with the voice of God from heaven speaking, *"This is my beloved Son, in whom I am well pleased"*.

Luke 4:1 describes Jesus as *"full of the Holy Spirit"* as He is led by the Spirit into the wilderness to be tested by the devil.

Jesus outlined steps to being *"full of the Holy Spirit"* in John 7:37-38.

> *Now on the last day, the great day of the feast, Jesus stood and cried out, saying, "If anyone is thirsty, let him come to Me and drink. 38He who believes in Me, as the Scripture said, 'From his innermost being will flow rivers of living water.'"*

John 7:37-38 (NASB)

I believe Jesus was saying this to us in the passage above.

1) We must desire Him (*thirst*)
2) We must repent of all known sin in our lives (*come to me*)
3) We must obey His command (*drink*)
4) We must use our faith and act upon the Word of God (*He who believes in me*)

The question is: "Are you filled to overflowing (outwardly) with the person of the Holy Spirit? Do others see the overflow? Do you want the overflow in your life?" Pursue the precious Holy Spirit and He will fill you with the power to minister in your daily life.

ACTIVATION
Holy Spirit Activations

(Read through all the instructions before you begin.)

1. Luke 17:21b states: *"Kingdom of God is within you."* Never look for the Kingdom of God anywhere but there, within.
2. Find a quiet un-interrupted place to approach the Holy Spirit.
3. Use instrumental worship music to quiet your soul. Preferably not songs you know or you will find yourself singing along. Soaking music can be found online.
4. Learn to silence your words, your desires, and your thoughts. Reaching inward to the place where God speaks to our inward man is crucial. This is the place God speaks to the Holy Spirit in us who teaches us and guides us. Silence enables the Holy Spirit to commune with us.
5. Come before the Lord with a deep sense of love and a deep sense of worship.
6. Humbly acknowledge that He is everything. Confess to Him that you are nothing.
7. Close your eyes to everything around you; ask the Holy Spirit to open the eyes of your spirit so that you may begin to know Him in a deeper way.
8. Sample Prayer: *Holy Spirit, I want to give myself to You. Give me the strength to give You everything. I want to know You! I want to be filled to overflow of Your Spirit which enables me to minister the things of God with power.*
9. Wait for His presence!
10. Once you experience His presence then remain silent to hear His voice.
11. Have a pad and pencil nearby to write down anything Holy Spirit speaks to you.

www.ingramcontent.com/pod-product-compliance
Lightning Source LLC
Chambersburg PA
CBHW052008090426
42741CB00008B/1609